Top Girls

Caryl Churchill is an award-winning playwright, whose plays are renowned for their striking influence upon contemporary British theatre practices. Indicative of her enduring impression upon the theatrical landscape, Churchill has won Obie Awards for her widely celebrated plays *Cloud 9* (1979), *Top Girls* (1982), *Serious Money* (1987) and *A Number* (2002). Further cementing her reputation as an outstanding playwright, in 2002 Churchill won an Obie Award for Lifetime Achievement and in 2010 was placed in the American Theatre Hall of Fame. She continues to produce innovative and provocative work, such as *Seven Jewish Children – a play for Gaza* (2009) and *Love and Information* (2012), and in January 2016 her latest full-length play, *Escaped Alone*, opened at the Royal Court Theatre to great acclaim. With an illustrious theatre career that spans four decades, Caryl Churchill is arguably more than just one of Britain's most revered female playwrights; she is one of Britain's most respected and groundbreaking working today.

Sophie Bush is a Lecturer in Performance at Sheffield Hallam University and has previously taught at the Universities of Sheffield, Huddersfield and Manchester Metropolitan. Her research and teaching interests lie in the history, practice and politics of contemporary British theatre. Her doctorate, on the work of Timberlake Wertenbaker, was awarded by the University of Sheffield in 2011, and in September 2013 her first book, *The Theatre of Timberlake Wertenbaker*, was published by Bloomsbury Methuen Drama. She is also the author of *My Mother Said I Never Should GCSE Student Edition* (Bloomsbury Methuen Drama, 2016) and *My Mother Said I Never Should GCSE Student Guide* (Bloomsbury Methuen Drama, 2016). She maintains an involvement with practical theatre-making, as director and devisor.

Also available from Bloomsbury Methuen Drama

Anthologies

Caryl Churchill Plays: 1
Caryl Churchill Plays: 2
Lives of the Great Poisoners
Plays by Women

Single play editions

Serious Money
Softcops and Fen
Top Girls

Top Girls

CARYL CHURCHILL

with commentary and notes by

SOPHIE BUSH

Series Editors: Jenny Stevens and Chris Megson

Bloomsbury Methuen Drama
An imprint of Bloomsbury Publishing Plc

B L O O M S B U R Y
LONDON · OXFORD · NEW YORK · NEW DELHI · SYDNEY

Bloomsbury Methuen Drama
An imprint of Bloomsbury Publishing Plc

Imprint previously known as Methuen Drama

50 Bedford Square	1385 Broadway
London	New York
WC1B 3DP	NY 10018
UK	USA

www.bloomsbury.com

BLOOMSBURY, METHUEN DRAMA and the Diana logo are registered trade marks of Bloomsbury Publishing Plc

Top Girls first published in 1982 by Methuen London
Student Edition first published in 1991 by Methuen Drama
Reissued with a new cover design 1994; with additional material and a new cover design 2005
Revised edition 2008; reissued with a new cover design 2009; reissued with corrections 2012
This edition with new material published 2018

British Library Cataloguing-in-Publication Data
A catalogue record for this book is available from the British Library.

ISBN:	PB:	978-1-3500-2857-9
	eBook:	978-1-3500-2859-3
	ePDF:	978-1-3500-2858-6

Library of Congress Cataloging-in-Publication Data
Names: Churchill, Caryl. author. | Bush, Sophie author of commentary.
Title: Top girls / Caryl Churchill ; with commentary and notes by Sophie Bush.
Description: London ; New York : Bloomsbury Methuen Drama, 2018. | Includes bibliographical references and index.
Identifiers: LCCN 2017029541| ISBN 9781350028579 (pb) | ISBN 9781350028586 (epdf)
Subjects: LCSH: Women—Social conditions—Drama.
Classification: LCC PR6053.H786 T6 2018 | DDC 822/.914—dc23 LC record available at https://lccn.loc.gov/2017029541

Series: Student Editions

Series design by Jocelyn Lucas
Cover images © Associated Press/Rex Shutterstock/Photographer Peter Morrison

Typeset by RefineCatch Limited, Bungay, Suffolk
Printed and bound in India

To find out more about our authors and books visit www.bloomsbury.com. Here you will find extracts, author interviews, details of forthcoming events and the option to sign up for our newsletters.

Contents

Chronology

Events from Churchill's life and career are shown in bold text; other theatrical events in standard type face; and social and political events in italics. Unless otherwise stated, the focus is on events in the UK.

1938   **Churchill born.**

1956   George Devine establishes London's Royal Court Theatre to seek out, develop and support new playwriting.

1956–9   **Churchill attends Lady Margaret Hall, Oxford University, to study English Language and Literature.**

1958   **Churchill's *Downstairs,* staged by a dramatic society at Oxford University, wins an award at the National Student Drama Festival.**

     Ann Jellicoe's *The Sport of My Mad Mother* at the Royal Court and Shelagh Delaney's *A Taste of Honey* produced by Joan Littlewood's Theatre Workshop at Theatre Royal, Stratford East.

1961   **Churchill marries barrister David Harter. (The couple go on to have three sons.)**

1962   **Churchill's first radio play *The Ants* broadcast on BBC Radio 3.**

     Ann Jellicoe's *The Knack* at the Royal Court.

1965   Edward Bond's *Saved* at the Royal Court.

     Barbara Castle becomes the first female minister of state (Minister of Transport).

1967   *Abortion and homosexuality are partially decriminalized.*

     The contraceptive pill becomes available on the NHS through Family Planning Clinics.

1967–72   **Churchill focuses on work for radio.**

1969   *The Divorce Reform Act enables men and women to file for divorce without proving either party is at fault. Divorce rates rise as a result.*

1970   *The Equal Pay Act makes it illegal to pay women less than men for the same work.*

1972   **Churchill's first professional stage production, *Owners*, at the Royal Court (Theatre Upstairs).**

1974   Joint Stock established.

        Contraception becomes more widely available through the NHS.

1974–5 **Churchill is the first female Writer in Residence at the Royal Court.**

1975   **Churchill's first play for the Royal Court (Theatre Downstairs) is *Objections to Sex and Violence*.**

        Monstrous Regiment established.

        Margaret Thatcher becomes leader of the Conservative Party.

        The Sex Discrimination Act makes it illegal to discriminate against women in work, education and training.

1976   **Churchill's *Light Shining in Buckinghamshire* developed with Joint Stock.**

        Churchill's *Vinegar Tom* developed with Monstrous Regiment.

        The Domestic Violence and Matrimonial Proceedings Act aims to protect and provide for victims of marital abuse.

1977   Pam Gems's *Queen Christina* produced by the Royal Shakespeare Company.

1979   **Churchill's *Cloud Nine* developed with Joint Stock.**

        Max Stafford-Clark becomes Artistic Director of the Royal Court.

The Conservative Party, led by Margaret Thatcher, wins the General Election, making Thatcher Britain's first female prime minister.

1980   **Churchill's *Three More Sleepless Nights* at the Soho Poly.**

1981   Timberlake Wertenbaker's *New Anatomies* produced by Women's Theatre Group.

Riots, first in Brixton, then in several British cities, are sparked by racial tensions, unemployment, social inequality and distrust of the police.

Ronald Reagan becomes fortieth President of the United States. He shares many of Thatcher's economic policies.

1982   **Churchill's *Top Girls* first produced at Royal Court (Theatre Downstairs), before transferring to Public Theatre, New York.**

Britain at war with Argentina over the Falkland Islands.

Britain in deep recession. Unemployment passes three million.

Greenham Common Women's Peace Camp established.

1983   **Churchill's *Fen* produced by Joint Stock.**

Thatcher's Conservative Party wins a second term in power, with an increased majority.

Millions take advantage of Thatcher's policy enabling people to buy their council houses, but this depletes the nation's social housing resource.

1984–5   *The government's response to the Miners' Strike increases class divide in British society.*

1985   Timberlake Wertenbaker's *The Grace of Mary Traverse* at the Royal Court.

1986   *Major national industries (such as those providing gas and oil, transport, and communication services) are privatized.*

Contexts

Women's liberation

Feminist or women's liberation movements can be categorized into several phases, usually referred to as 'waves'. First-wave feminism covers the nineteenth- and twentieth-century women's movements, whose main goal was to secure women's right to vote in political elections, a concept also known as female, women's or universal suffrage. In Britain, this right was granted to women over the age of thirty in 1918, but younger women did not gain access to the same voting rights as men until 1928. The first wave of feminist movements also contributed to other advances for women, such as enabling their entry into certain jobs from which they had previously been barred, such as the legal profession and accountancy, and securing the right for married women to own their own property and to file for divorce on the same grounds as men.

The second wave of feminism is usually dated from the 1960s to the 1980s and as such is the most crucial to consider in relation to Churchill's work. Many of the ideas that drove this movement originated in the United States, but were quickly picked up and developed in Britain and other parts of the world. Whilst first-wave feminism had focused its attention on big 'P' Political and legal issues, the second wave saw the equal importance of small 'p' or 'personal politics', and campaigned around a wide range of issues, including women's access to contraception and abortion, resistance to domestic and sexual violence, and the examination of women's roles within the family and the workplace. In the UK, many of these campaigns resulted in changes to the law, including the Abortion Act (1967), the Equal Pay Act (1970), the Sex Discrimination Act (1975) and the Domestic Violence and Matrimonial Proceedings Act (1976). As well as lobbying governments for these changes, the movement also undertook extensive 'grassroots' activism, organizing 'consciousness-raising' groups and sessions for women who wanted to discover more about sexual inequality and the ways they could combat it. There was also a big increase in publishing (of books, journals and journalism) by, for and about women, further increasing the visibility of women and women's issues to a general readership.

Whilst many aims were shared by women throughout this second wave of feminism, there were also several distinguishable positions within the broader movement, each of which emphasized slightly different aspects of the cause. For example:

Essentialist feminism

One school of feminism has been termed 'essentialist' because it focuses on defining and valuing certain qualities as specifically or 'essentially' female, and celebrating natural processes associated with the female body, such as pregnancy, childbirth and menstruation. This form of feminism is not overtly obvious in *Top Girls*, but resonates with the moment in Act Two, Scene One, where Angie licks Kit's menstrual blood off her finger and instructs Kit to do the same 'when I get mine' (98).

Bourgeois feminism

This is the sort of feminism encapsulated by Marlene's character and, to a lesser extent, the women we see working alongside her at the Top Girls agency. Unlike essentialist feminism, which celebrates women's difference from men, bourgeois feminism denies such differences exist or are meaningful, in order to stress the equal footing on which women can and should compete with men (and with each other) to reach the top positions of social and professional status.

Socialist or materialist feminism

This is another perspective that seeks to highlight difference; not the innate differences between men and women flagged up by essentialist feminism, but rather the socially and culturally constructed differences between different women and groups of women. This perspective asks women to consider, and try to fight against, the inequalities of opportunity available to them, depending on factors such as their social class or racial demographic. The play highlights these conditions, which allow particular women like Marlene to enjoy individual success without ensuring the success of many more women like Joyce and Angie, whose circumstances mean they are unable to access such privilege.

Further reading

The following sources provide more detail on different aspects of feminism, and some are particularly useful in explaining their relationship with theatre and performance:

Case, Sue-Ellen (2008), *Feminism and Theatre*. Reissued edition. Basingstoke: Palgrave Macmillan.

Goodman, Lizbeth (2003), *Contemporary Feminist Theatre: To Each Her Own*. Abingdon: Routledge.

Haslanger, Sally et al. (2012), 'Topics in feminism'. *Stanford Encyclopedia of Philosophy* [online], 28 November . Available at: https://plato. stanford.edu/entries/feminism-topics/; accessed 14 April 2017.

No author (n.d.), 'Feminism: A collection of TED Talks (and more) on the topic of feminism'. *TED* [online]. Available at: https://www.ted.com/ topics/feminism; accessed 14 April 2017.

Sisterhood and After Research Team (n.d.), 'What is a feminist?' *British Library* [online]. Available at: https://www.bl.uk/sisterhood/articles/ what-is-a-feminist; accessed 14 April 2017.

Solga, Kim (2016), *Theatre & Feminism*. Basingstoke: Palgrave Macmillan.

Walters, Margaret (2005), *Feminism: A Very Short Introduction*. Oxford: Oxford University Press.

Margaret Thatcher and British politics

Top Girls is haunted throughout by the figure of Margaret Thatcher, the UK's first female prime minister, in office from 1979 to 1990. In fact, director Max Stafford-Clark cites Thatcher's election as the major stimulus that prompted Churchill to develop this play over other ideas she was mulling over at the time (see interview below). For some women, Thatcher's ability to rise to the top of a male-dominated political system, despite the prejudices she encountered because of her gender, was inspiring. For others, her individual success was meaningless, as she denied the value of feminism to her own achievements, and did little to advance the position of other women, either within the political sphere or in society at large. She famously promoted no other women within her government, except for the unelected peer Baroness Young, who she briefly made Leader of the House of Lords.

Thatcher introduced several economic and social policies associated with the theory of monetarism, which posits that financial markets operate best when left to their own devices, rather than under state regulation. Broadly speaking, these policies involved a reduction of public spending on welfare and services, including the privatization of what had hitherto been state-owned providers of utilities, transport and communications services, alongside a reduction in state regulation of financial institutions. These economic policies also matched Thatcher's ideological belief in individualism and meritocracy. These are concepts which state that individual people, rather than their societies, are responsible for how much they can achieve, and that an extensive welfare state is not only a drain on the nation's resources but potentially a 'crutch' that prevents certain sections of the population from pulling their weight or achieving their potential. We can see this attitude still prevalent today in the demonization of those living on benefits by certain sections of our media and government. Whilst Thatcher's policies partially succeeded in boosting the British economy, particularly in the capital, this was achieved at the cost of a widening gap between the richest and poorest members of society, and increased homelessness and unemployment, particularly in northern and rural areas of the UK.

It is therefore easy to see why Thatcher is such a divisive figure in the pivotal argument between Marlene and Joyce in Act Three of the play. Like Thatcher, Marlene has succeeded in a male-dominated profession, due to a combination of her own resourcefulness and a lack of regard for those she has had to step on to get there. Like Thatcher, her personal success has given her a fervent belief in individualism and meritocracy. This is most evident in Marlene's line: 'I don't believe in class. Anyone can do anything if they've got what it takes' (158). Consequently, Marlene (like Thatcher) does not see it as her social responsibility to help or support women (or men) whose personal attributes or circumstances leave them less able to succeed. Contrastingly, Joyce serves as a striking reminder of the class Marlene no longer believes in, and the society Thatcher claimed did not exist. In a much-quoted interview with the traditional women's lifestyle magazine *Woman's Own*, Thatcher pronounced: 'There is no such thing as society. There are individual men and women and there are families' (23 September 1987).

Further reading

The sources listed below provide further discussion of Thatcher's policies in general, whilst some focus in particular on their effect on women. You might also want to look at some of the coverage and response to Margaret Thatcher's death in 2013, which ranged from solemn eulogies to jubilant street parties. Think about what clues these responses can give us about the kind of leader Thatcher was and the effect she had on different parts of the country.

Another thing to think about is the position of female leaders today. You might consider figures such as Hillary Clinton, Theresa May, Angela Merkel and Nicola Sturgeon. To what extent does their gender impact on their leadership or the way it is discussed and represented in the media? Do they face any gender-specific problems or challenges?

Ball, James, (2013), 'The Thatcher effect: What changed and what stayed the same'. *Guardian* [online], 12 April. Available at: https://www. theguardian.com/politics/2013/apr/12/thatcher-britain; accessed 14 April 2017.

Childs, Sarah (2013), 'Thatcher's gender trouble: Ambivalence and the Thatcher legacy'. *Political Studies Association* [online], 17 April. Available at: https://www.psa.ac.uk/political-insight/blog/ thatcher%e2%80%99s-gender-trouble-ambivalence-and-thatcher-legacy; accessed 14 April 2017.

Farrell, Stephen and Colin Hay (eds) (2014), *The Legacy of Thatcherism: Assessing and Exploring Thatcherite Social and Economic Policies.* Oxford: Oxford University Press.

Hadley, Louisa and Elizabeth Ho (eds) (2010), *Thatcher and After: Margaret Thatcher and her Afterlife in Contemporary Culture.* Basingstoke: Palgrave Macmillan.

Jackson, Ben and Robert Saunders (eds) (2012), *Making Thatcher's Britain*. Cambridge: Cambridge University Press.

Lakhani, Nina (2013), 'Margaret Thatcher: How much did The Iron Lady do for the UK's women?' *Independent* [online], 8 April. Available at: http://www.independent.co.uk/news/uk/politics/margaret-thatcher-how-much-did-the-iron-lady-do-for-the-uks-women-8564631.html; accessed 14 April 2017.

LSE Public Policy Group (2013), 'The legacy of Margaret Thatcher'. *London: LSE Public Policy Group* [online]. Available at: http://blogs.lse.ac.uk/politicsandpolicy/files/2013/05/Thatcher-final.pdf; accessed 14 April 2017.

Murray, Jenni (2013), 'What did Margaret Thatcher do for women?' *Guardian* [online], 9 April. Available at: https://www.theguardian.com/politics/2013/apr/09/margaret-thatcher-women; accessed 14 April 2017.

Seldon, Anthony and Daniel Collings (1999), *Britain under Thatcher*. Abingdon: Routledge.

Vinen, Richard (2010), *Thatcher's Britain: The Politics and Social Upheaval of the 1980s*. London: Simon and Schuster.

Caryl Churchill and the British theatre scene

Caryl Churchill was born in London in 1938. Her father was a political cartoonist and her mother combined acting work with raising her daughter. Churchill had a comfortable, middle-class upbringing, mostly in Canada, where the family moved whilst she was still a young child, and where Churchill lived until she returned to England to study English Language and Literature at Oxford University in 1956.

It was at university that Churchill's playwriting took off. Several of her early plays were staged by student dramatic societies and one, *Downstairs*, won an award at the National Student Drama Festival in 1958. However, her decision to marry and start a family shortly after leaving university limited her ability to immediately capitalize on this success within the realms of the professional theatre. Instead, during the 1960s, Churchill wrote mainly for radio, a medium which is less demanding of a writer's time than the stage, due to the lengthy stretches a playwright may want or need to spend in the rehearsal room during the first production of a new stage play. These early works for radio foreground Churchill's developing ability to create arresting imagery through an experimental approach to language, alongside her talent for interweaving intense and recognizable human relationships with the much broader political, social and environmental concerns, which are impacted by and impact upon them.

Theatrical collectives

In the 1970s, Churchill became much more engaged with theatre and with politics, largely through work with theatrical 'collectives'. These companies sought to challenge established theatre's directorial and management structures by operating in a less hierarchical way, and promoting ensemble practice and shared decision-making. Many of these companies focussed their work on specific political issues of the day. For example, several were established with the primary purpose of promoting women's work and concerns. These included Monstrous Regiment (est. 1975), who Churchill worked with on her 1976 production, *Vinegar Tom*. Others were formed from a primarily socialist perspective. One such was Joint Stock, established in 1974 by David Aukin, William Gaskill, David Hare and Max Stafford-Clark. This company developed new work through several weeks of collaborative research and workshops with a playwright, director and actors. They worked with Churchill to create *Light Shining in Buckinghamshire* in 1976 and *Cloud Nine* in 1979, establishing a long-standing and fruitful working relationship between Churchill and Stafford-Clark, who directed both productions.

The Royal Court Theatre

London's Royal Court Theatre was established in 1956 by the actor, director and theatre manager George Devine, to seek out, develop and support the best new British and international playwriting, and expose audiences to the most exciting and up-to-date theatrical developments. This institution's willingness to take risks has played a vitally important role in putting seminal – and often controversial

– works, such as John Osborne's *Look Back in Anger* (1956), Edward Bond's *Saved* (1965), and Sarah Kane's *Blasted* (1995) in front of British audiences, and in shaping the careers of many key figures in British playwriting, including Churchill, Kane, Timberlake Wertenbaker, David Hare, Martin Crimp and numerous others. As well as producing her best-known work such as *Top Girls* (1982) and *Serious Money* (1987), the Court produced Churchill's first professional stage play, *Owners*, in 1972 and between 1974 and 1975 employed her as their first female Writer in Residence. They have continued to produce much of Churchill's work to the present day, including *Love and Information* (2012), *Ding Dong the Wicked* (2013), and *Escaped Alone* (2016).

Max Stafford-Clark

Max Stafford-Clark was the Artistic Director of the Royal Court between 1979 and 1993. Having previously co-founded the company Joint Stock, he applied their collaborative creative process (now known as the 'Joint Stock method') to a number of his productions for the Royal Court, though not *Top Girls*. Under Stafford-Clark's tenure, the Royal Court paid increased attention to promoting and developing new writing by women, such as Churchill, Wertenbaker, Louise Page and April de Angelis. As well as directing the original production of *Top Girls* in 1982, Stafford-Clark directed major revivals of the play in 1991 and 2011, making him uniquely placed to comment on its continued relevance over this period. The following interview was conducted by Sophie Bush on 17 February 2017.

SB: What were your initial impressions on reading the script of *Top Girls*?

MSC: Well, I have to say, my memory is rather different from Caryl's. It could be that the truth lies somewhere outside both our recollections, as it is some time ago. But I recollect that she sent me a script, and at that point, the first scene was a series of monologues that had not been intercut. And we went for a walk, and I said, 'look Caryl, I think it's very good, but with fourteen or fifteen characters, it's totally out of the question'. And she said, 'actually what we can do is double up with that – Dull Gret goes with Angie', and she laid out that you could do it with seven actors. Anyway, that was the realization that you could do it [by] doubling or trebling.

SB: I've read that that doubling has been credited to you, rather than something that was integral to Churchill's conception of the play, as with the doubling in *Cloud Nine*.

MSC: I think that on the first occasion, she was very flexible about it. And it was quite clear that it could go this way or could go that way. And I think I laid out just one possibility.

SB: It's interesting that it wasn't the original intention, as there seem to be interesting parallels between the characters the same actors play within the first and second and third acts.

MSC: With Dull Gret and Angie there are, but not so much with the others – with Griselda and Nell, for example.

SB: Was it a project that you'd discussed with Churchill, prior to receiving a draft of it on your desk?

MSC: We'd discussed a number of possible projects, but I think that Thatcher's ascension to power really pushed her to take on this one.

SB: What are the biggest challenges that the play presents to a director?

MSC: Well, obviously, the first challenge was how you do that surreal first scene. In fact, I approached it totally, as it were, naturalistically. Thinking, who would be at home at this dinner party? Well, obviously, the pope. Who would not be at home? Dull Gret would be overawed and could behave badly – eat the bread rolls. The way the women interact is determined by class and experience. We went into all kinds of things – how much Marlene has paid for the dinner. And of course, apart from the first scene (chronologically, the last scene is the first scene), the play has a through timeline. Marlene is promoted; she gives the dinner party; she comes in hung over on the Monday morning. Meanwhile, Kit and Angie have their scene in the back garden on the Sunday.

Angie resolves to run away. Then you have to make up facts. She probably raids Joyce's purse that she has left in the kitchen overnight and takes a tenner. She probably gets up at five o'clock to get the first bus into Ipswich, changes buses there. I mean, how does she know where Marlene's office is?

SB: So those economic and material circumstances were really integral to your finding your way through the play? Was that helpful for the actors – to have something very tangible to cling on to?

MSC: Yes, very much so.

SB: The critical response to that first production was fairly mixed, with some very positive reviews and some that absolutely failed to understand what have subsequently been recognized as the play's most innovative and interesting features.

MSC: Absolutely correct. The play was not a huge success. It did respectably at the Royal Court. Full on a cheap Monday, full on a Friday and Saturday, dipped in the middle of the week. But when we got to New York, Joe Papp billed it as a London hit and it packed out the Newman Theatre, which seats 300.[1] And then when we returned to London, we could justifiably say it was a New York hit. So, it accrued a reputation, rather than achieving one straight away.

SB: And with those reviews that didn't really understand it, did you suspect there would be a bit of a reassessment of that?

MSC: Yes. Caryl describes herself as a socialist feminist, and certainly the perspective of the play is very important, so I thought it would catch on.

SB: I read that after the first night, you wrote that the play had achieved peer approval; potentially critical disapproval, but a sense that immediately the industry were very excited about it.

MSC: Actors, yes. But it caught the critics on the hop a bit – the structure of it. Irving Wardle, the critic for the *Times*, said that the

---

1   Also known as the Public Theatre.

nightmare was always going to the theatre and missing the ball completely. That actually, we didn't spot *The Birthday Party*. And it was a little bit the same with *Top Girls*. But by the time we came back from New York, the critics had caught on.

SB: I also read that you once said it was the best play you'd ever directed. I'm not sure if you meant that it was the best script you'd ever worked on, or the production you were most satisfied with, but either way, what made it so, and has it retained that sense of being at the top of your work?

MSC: Yes, certainly. I mean, as I'm afraid, we're all shallow, a success like *Top Girls* or *Our Country's Good* means that that goes to the top of your list. I mean there are plays I am very proud of, plays that were never hits (*Rat in the Skull* by Ron Hutchinson, for instance, and more recently, *Crouch, Touch, Pause, Engage*), but *Top Girls* – I think I was actually referring to the script itself – that it made a political contribution to the debate on the state of the nation, as well as a theatrical one. It was incredibly apposite. I mean, I always knew from *Light Shining in Buckinghamshire* onwards that Caryl had, not just a first-rate intelligence, but a theatrical intuition, that's quite remarkable. I pride myself that I'm quite good at editing, but she would say, 'oh look, you can go from that line here to that – you don't need that'. And I would think, yes, of course, why didn't I see that? So her theatrical brain was a pleasure to be with.

SB: And you directed – as well as the initial production in 1982 – major revivals in 1991 and 2011?

MSC: Yes, that's absolutely right, because in the first production, Lesley Manville played Griselda and Nell, and then she came back and played Marlene.

SB: Do you have any recollection of any major differences, either in the way you approached the play for those different periods, or in the way it was received?

MSC: Well, certainly the world had changed. And whereas in the 1980s there were pictures in *Vogue* of women in shoulder pads and power-dressing, in the early nineties, it was all mothers and babies. So there was more of that focus. In the first scene, what all the women have in common is that they've all sacrificed their relationships with children, or not had children, in order to expedite their careers. Or Dull Gret's children are killed, rather than given up.

SB: So there was more of a sort of *fetishization* of motherhood in the 1990s?

MSC: More of a *celebration*.

SB: And does that make Marlene even less of a sympathetic character?

MSC: I wouldn't say it made her less sympathetic, but it sharpened the audience's perception of what she'd had to give up. Also, of course, by the nineties, there was more of a perspective on Thatcher: people had taken sides. It's interesting that the last line is Angie's 'frightening', which always in Caryl's mind referred to the decade ahead that was going to be frightening. But I saw a production in Bulgaria, in Sofia, where 'frightening' clearly referred to not what was ahead, but what had been.

SB: That sort of national difference is interesting.

MSC: Caryl talks about a German production where there was a huge swimming pool downstage, and all the scenes had to be played upstage of it. The swimming pool wasn't used at all – and clearly it cost thousands and thousands of euros – until the last moment, after 'frightening', Marlene pushes Angie into the pool and drowns her!

SB: And you did the play even more recently, in 2011?

MSC: That's right – at Chichester. Chichester audiences are, on the one hand, quite elderly, and therefore quite conservative, and on the other hand, they see a lot of theatre, so you would not think the innovations of *Top Girls* would have thrown them. But I remember on the first preview there were twenty-one walk-outs after the first scene, and one gentleman said, 'I don't know what this is about – just drunken women talking!' And then, on my left, there was a gentleman in immaculate corduroys and his wife, and when the lights came up for the second scene, which is Angie and Kit in their back yard – on hay bales they were sitting on, and the dinner party cleared away, of course – and as the lights came up on them, he turned to his wife and said 'oh God, where on earth do you suppose we are now?' So even years later, the play can still provoke and make the audience work hard. When we played in Warwick – a university town – one comment on their Twitter feed said 'this was the worst play I have ever seen', and another said 'thank God this play is still as pertinent today as when it was written'. So it was far more contentious in 2011 than I had anticipated.

SB: Do you think it has dated at all, or is it every bit as pertinent?

MSC: I think it is still pertinent subject matter. Caryl has moved on structurally, but I think the content of the play is as sharp as ever. Certainly, critically, the response to the 2011 production was overwhelmingly approving. Much more so than it had been on previous occasions.

SB: Did you change anything in the staging, setting or direction of those productions, or were they quite similar?

MSC: I had a different designer, of course, but I was always keen that for the first scene, because the ladies enter a restaurant, that the restaurant was, as it were, in the basement, that each character is clearly presented as they enter, and so we kept that from the first production.

SB: What was it about that image?

MSC: It was that each character enters rather excitingly, so you see the pope, you see Griselda, and think 'who on earth is she?'. Or Dull Gret enters with her sword – these dramatic pictures tell the story.

SB: Before you get the context for them?

MSC: Before you get the words.

I think in retrospect, because it's only a perspective you can have in retrospect, that the play really established Caryl's eminence as *the* major writer. And I would say that after Pinter's demise, she is without question, the most important voice writing today.

SB: It's partly to do with that constant reinvention of style, isn't it? It's remarkable that new, exciting writers – male and female – who you'd think might want to disparage older writers, always cite Churchill as a major influence.

MSC: That's correct, though I think there are those who have swallowed the Caryl Churchill songbook without really digesting it! But her willingness to experiment and to uncover the new is absolutely a positive influence. Although, I think Caryl went through a phase where she was really pissed off about the theatre. If you write in order to change the world – to achieve some kind of political influence – and then, actually, the nation elects David Cameron, then you can hardly be said to have succeeded. So in one sense, she is enormously successful; on another level, I think the theatre is not the potent instrument for change that she once hoped she was writing for, and I think there were a number of 'anti-plays' like *Blue Heart* and *This is a Chair* that dramatically indicate her disenchantment with the stage.

Further reading

The following sources provide some useful context about this period in British theatre and the institutions, individuals and companies discussed in this section:

Billington, Michael (2007), *State of the Nation: British Theatre since 1945*. London: Faber and Faber.

Little, Ruth and Emily McLaughlin (2007), *The Royal Court Theatre Inside Out*. London: Oberon Books.

McKeown, Maeve (2008), 'Max Stafford-Clark: Education Resource Pack'. *Out of Joint* [online]. Available at: http://www.outofjoint.co.uk/wp-content/uploads/2010/09/Max-Stafford-Clark-Workpack.pdf; accessed 14 April 2017.

No author (n.d.), 'History'. *Royal Court* [online]. Available at: https://royalcourttheatre.com/about/history/; accessed 14 April 2017.

Roberts, Philip (1999), *The Royal Court Theatre and the Modern Stage*. Cambridge: Cambridge University Press.

Roberts, Philip and Max Stafford-Clark (2007), *Taking Stock: The Theatre of Max Stafford-Clark*. London: Nick Hern Books.

Critical response, recognition and influence[2]

There were several extremely positive reviews of the play's first
production, by both male and female critics, in a range of publications.
John Elsom (*Mail on Sunday*) found the play 'impressive', 'virile' and
'cunningly constructed', and praised its success in 'seizing our times
by the scruff of the neck and shaking out the cant'. Robert Cushman
(*Observer*) applauded the play's ability to be both 'personal' and
'polygonal' (many-sided), and cited it as one of 'the two most
interesting new plays of the year' (alongside Louise Page's *Salonika*).
However, in doing so, he signalled it as notable that both these plays
were written by women, adding somewhat patronisingly that a 'chap
has to take notice'. A mild sexism is also implicit in his (and many
other critics') reference to 'Miss Churchill' (as it is conventional to
refer to writers by their full name or surname only, without a title,
which in this case deliberately signals Churchill's gender and youth)
and in his closing comments that congratulate Max Stafford-Clark on
his direction and 'wonder how he felt in rehearsals' alongside the all-
female cast and playwright.

In *Time Out*, Ann McFerran called it a 'rich, ambitious play' and a
'theatrical first', drawing attention to the play's innovative structure of
an 'exquisite and stylish first scene', which 'opens into scenes of crisp
social realism, Bondian in their resonance and clarity'. This
comparison to the playwright Edward Bond is significant as it situates
Churchill within a dramatic heritage that traditionally, at this time,
was reserved for men. Cushman makes another comparison,
suggesting that 'Churchill also does for overlapping dialogue on stage
what Robert Altman has done in the movies'. Other critics were keen
to signal Churchill's significance directly, with Clive Hirschhorn
(*Sunday Express*) professing that the play 'reinforces Caryl Churchill's
status as one of our most original and exciting dramatists', and Bryan
Roberts (*Spectator*) describing her as 'one of our best writers'.

Not all reviews were so enthusiastic, however. Whilst Rosalind
Carne (*Financial Times*) described the play as structurally ambitious,
'juggling simultaneously, and most effectively, with historical time',

---

2   The reviews quoted in this section are collated in *London Theatre Record*, 26 Aug–8 Sept
    1982.

other critics found fault with its structural logic. Kenneth Hurren (*What's On in London*) felt there were only 'occasional thin and vagrant parallels' between the first act and the rest of the play, and that though 'most of what happens is interesting', the play 'never really begins to cohere, and the piece as a whole is rather less than the sum of its parts'. Likewise, Nicholas de Jongh (*Guardian*) complained that 'Miss Churchill never really convinces us that this dramatic back cloth to the play [Act One] has any developed relationship or ironic contrast with what follows'. Elsewhere, there was disagreement over whether the first act was the play's high point or its biggest failing. Harold Atkins (*Daily Telegraph*) argued the former, describing Act One as a 'brilliant fantasia', after which the play's 'style swerves away absolutely', leaving 'a medium key story' ending with 'a dramatic whisper'. On the other hand, Rosalie Horner (*Daily Express*) felt that it 'is not until the first scene of Act Two that the play says anything cogent'.

Many critics (Atkins, Cushman, Hirschhorn, Roberts) described the play as explicitly feminist without attaching overt negativity to this term. However, Roberts was glad to find that whilst the 'play is feminist, all right', 'it is an entertaining, sometimes painful and often funny play and not a mere tract', and Atkins seemed relieved that its presentation of feminist ideas was 'unobtrusive'. Only Tim Satchell (*Daily Mail*) expressed direct hostility to the term, complaining that 'the whiff of feminism hangs uncomfortably over' the play. Meanwhile, Milton Shulman (*Standard*) dismissed Churchill's Act One explorations of historical sexism and misogyny as no different from general acts of barbarity committed during these periods, and considered it risible that 'Miss Churchill would have us believe that similar pressures and hardships are inflicted on career women of today'. Consequently, he condemned the play as something 'predictable' and 'trite', which 'does not survive a moment's logical or intellectual analysis'.

Other reviewers criticized the play for not being clear enough about its message. Francis King (*Sunday Telegraph*) described it as 'an inchoate play, seemingly written on the principle "I don't know what I think until I get it onto paper"'. Similarly, Hurren suggested that 'Ms Churchill writes vivaciously, and clearly has a lot on her mind about the status of women and the shifting roles of the sexes but, like some of her previous work, it all seems not so much a play as a cry for help in getting her mind sorted out'.

Many critics were thrown by Churchill's unusual overlapping dialogue. Dick Vosburgh (*Punch*) claims he 'missed a lot of' the play's first scene because of it, and King found that 'many passages are unintelligible because of the author's directions in the text that they should be spoken simultaneously'. Roberts, in an otherwise positive review, found the device 'an irritating conceit [. . .] which serves no purpose, real or symbolic'. However, Robert Warden (*Event*) described the opening scene as 'astonishing in its continuous flow of interruptions'. Hurren had a positive response to the overlapping dialogue in Marlene and Joyce's Act Three argument, but was 'less certain about the desirability of applying this technique to the dinner-party conversation'.

Also of note are the ways in which several male reviewers refer to women's speech and women characters within the play. Satchell describes a 'silly secretary' that Marlene interviews, and Atkins refer to 'shallow girls running an employment agency'. Satchell also references women who 'scream and battle out the recriminations', and King suggests that as they 'screech simultaneously at each other across a kitchen-table, their arguments are often unintelligible'. Shulman describes women who 'chatter about their lives, never listening to each other'. The derisive and insulting adjectives used here to dismiss women's voices fit into a much broader pattern of sexism, as discussed by the Classics scholar Mary Beard.[3]

The clearest example of this tendency is in Dick Vosburgh's review for *Punch*, which is written as a dialogue with a psychiatrist:

Psychiatrist: And what exactly is troubling you, Mr Vosburgh?

Vosburgh: Well Doc, Sheridan Morley is on holiday and I'm standing in for him at Punch, and last night I . . . think I went

---

3   Beard, Mary (2014), 'The public voice of women'. *London Review of Books* [online], 36(6), 20 March, pp. 11–14. Available at: https://www.lrb.co.uk/v36/n06/mary-beard/the-public-voice-of-women; accessed 15 March 2014.

to the Royal Court and saw a play by Caryl Churchill called
TOP GIRLS.

P: What do you mean you *think*? Why aren't you sure you
saw this play?

V: Well, because it . . . it opened in a restaurant where
Marlene, a pushy modern executive was welcoming her
guests: [. . .] It seems there was a long, very funny scene in
which they all talked about their lives, only I missed a lot of
it. You see there was a lot of overlapping dialogue because
the director, Max Stafford-Clark, would obviously have
given his hyphen to have directed Citizen Kane. And there
was a scene between two kids – a teenage girl and a younger
one, only they're both played by grown-ups . . .

P: You say this was a play? It sounds more like a revue.

V: I know. [. . .] Then we're suddenly into what looks like
a slice of a fascinating play about the pushy modern
executive and her sister and the teenager we met earlier . . .

P: Mr Vosburgh, will you please take this sedative. You are
not a well man – there couldn't *possibly* be such a play as
you describe!

Vosburgh is writing for comic effect, but even so, his implication –
that Churchill's play is a symptom of a diseased or hysterical mind
– is concerning (and if we were to consider this in relation to the
disturbing scene between Betty and her Doctor in Churchill's earlier
play *Vinegar Tom*, the effect is even more chilling).

Another notable review is Benedict Nightingale's *New Statesman*
piece, which devotes fewer words to discussing the play itself, than
it does to detailing the paucity of women's playwriting before this
time. 'Most of you, like most of me, must have wondered why
women's contribution to British drama should have been so slim',
Nightingale begins, continuing:

I myself recently brought out a paperback discussing our
20th-century theatre by the somewhat glib device of
discussing 50 interesting and/or significant plays, and,

though I spent some furrowed hours reassessing Jellicoe and
Delaney, I couldn't in all conscience include a single one by
a woman.

Nightingale's article shows a genuine attempt to understand why,
historically, so few women had written plays that he might value,
and he tries hard to avoid sexist criticisms. He speculates about the
off-putting effect of the 'sweaty male world of telegrams and anger,
with auditions, meetings, readings, wrangles', but concludes that
many women 'would have been perfectly capable of standing up to
the male establishment'. He also discusses a theory that:

> there's something in the female temperament innately alien
> to the dramatic form: theatrical work is too external, too
> rectilinear, too rigidly structured a means of expression for
> creative minds that tend to be subtler, more curvilinear, and
> therefore better suited to the novel; and the reason that more
> women are now beginning to write for the stage is that the
> old, mechanical 'well-made play' is in decline and a more
> flexible and elastic style of drama is on the rise.

However, he acknowledges that this interpretation 'could be accused
of propagating sexist attitudes in a fake-flattering way'. Eventually,
he comes to the rather unsatisfactory conclusion that perhaps
'theatre, while not excluding female writers de jure, was de facto a
sort of no go area' which women 'did not even consider entering'.
'Tradition', he hypothesizes, 'brain-washed, rather than positively
browbeat, would-be playwrights into writing novels or staying
mum; and only a few, and those not the most talented, broke the
unwritten rules'. But, Nightingale considers, that situation is now
changing:

> I don't know whether something has happened to the
> theatrical establishment, to the drama, or to women
> themselves; but something has happened. I find myself
> reviewing a rapidly increasing amount of work by female
> dramatists, few less than promising and several much more
> than that. The past few months alone have seen plays by
> Catharine Hayes, Gilly Fraser, Natasha Morgan, Melissa
> Murray, Olwen Wymark, Ellen Dryden, Claire Luckham, Sue

Townsend, Bryony Lavery, Nell Dunn, Angela Huth, Elaine
Morgan, Carol Williams, that hive of industry which calls
itself Pam Gems, Louise Page . . . and, just last week, Caryl
Churchill, the most accomplished of them all.

It is significant that, despite the long list of female dramatists
mentioned here, it is Churchill's *Top Girls* that has finally prompted
Nightingale to publish this reassessment of the importance of
women's playwriting, citing the play as 'articulate, eloquent, alive,
proof in itself that we can no longer patronise women playwrights as
peripheral'.

Nightingale's blind spot towards women's playwriting is not
unusual. Whilst it might seem quite remarkable that he could not
bring himself to include work by Jellicoe or Delaney (or Gems or
Churchill herself) in his volume, his decision is fairly representative
of the tendency to dismiss the significance of women's writing. This
is evident in several more contemporary surveys, which include
Churchill's play alongside very few, if any, other plays by women,
such as the National Theatre's 100 most significant plays of the
twentieth century (2000), Michael Billington's 101 greatest plays of
all time (*Guardian*, 2 September 2015), and the *Telegraph*'s 15 best
plays of all time (28 April 2014). In fact, even the commentary to the
previous student edition of this play text (first published in 1991, but
revised as recently as 2008) began with the comment 'Like Pope
Joan, Caryl Churchill is something of a heresy. She is a major
contemporary British dramatist and a woman', and considered that
the 'fact that it is a woman playwright who is experimenting in
dramatic form enlivens critical analysis'. It then goes on to
contextualize Churchill's writing only within a male-authored canon.

Awards

In the 1982/3 Off-Broadway Theater Awards ('Obies'), *Top Girls*
won Churchill the Obie for 'Outstanding Writer' and both its English
and American casts were recognized for 'Outstanding Ensemble
Performances'. In 1983, the play saw her classified as a 'runner-up'
for the Susan Smith Blackburn Prize (an award she won the following
year for her play *Fen*, and again in 1987 for *Serious Money*).

Artistic influence

In a chapter of *The Cambridge Companion to Caryl Churchill* 'On Churchill's influences' (pp. 163–79), Dan Rebellato also charts Churchill's *influence*, detailing his own correspondence with a number of contemporary playwrights who cite Churchill's example as paramount to their own careers. Amongst them, Dennis Kelly, Anthony Neilson and David Eldridge all praise her constantly (re)inventive work, especially her experimentation with form (164).[4]

Rebellato suggests that we can see Churchill's influence not only when it is directly cited but also as evidenced through other theatrical works that adopt devices she pioneered. For example, in the temporal shifts in Tom Stoppard's *Arcadia* (1993), Shelagh Stevenson's *An Experiment with an Air Pump* (1998) and Ravenhill's *Mother Clap's Molly House* (2001) (to this list we could add Sarah Kane's *Blasted* (1995) and Timberlake Wertenbaker's *After Darwin* (1998)); and in the bringing together of famous women from biblical stories in Sarah Daniels's *Beside Herself* (1990). However, for Rebellato, 'even more significantly, Churchill's influence has been in being the woman playwright who [has "broken through"]' into a male-dominated establishment: 'a formidable role-model for many other women playwrights', but 'no longer defined and confined by her gender' (174). Timberlake Wertenbaker confirms this assessment, writing in a letter of 1984, held in her archive: 'women playwrights are helped by women models. Caryl Churchill has broken new ground for women by extending the boundaries of subject'. However, Mary Luckhurst (2015) warns against overemphasizing Churchill's influence in this regard to the exclusion of other women writers.

---

4   Rebellato also refers to several published articles that assert this influence, including these two pieces, available online: Benedict, David (1997), 'The mother of reinvention'. *Independent* [online], 19 April. Available at: http://www.independent.co.uk/arts-entertainment/books/arts-books-the-mother-of-reinvention-1267902.html; accessed 16 April 2017; Ravenhill, Mark (2008), 'She made us raise our game'. *Guardian* [online], 3 September. Available at: https://www.theguardian.com/stage/2008/sep/03/carylchurchill.theatre; accessed 16 April 2017.

The play today

Since its premiere, *Top Girls* has received numerous professional productions across the globe. Recent UK revivals include:

2000	Battersea Arts Centre, London (dir. Thea Sharrock) and UK tour.
2002	Oxford Stage Company production (dir. Thea Sharrock) at Aldwych Theatre, London.
2006	Watford Palace Theatre (dir. Kirsty Davis).
2011–12	Out of Joint/Chichester Festival Theatre production (dir. Max Stafford-Clark) at Chichester Festival Theatre, Trafalgar Studios, London and UK tour.

As Stafford-Clark has mentioned, reviews of the 2011–12 production were overwhelmingly positive. Assessing the play long after its importance has been widely recognized, we see none of the confusion with which critics greeted the original production. Instead, we hear it called a 'modern classic' (Charles Spencer, *Daily Telegraph*) and 'one of the canonical plays of the late twentieth century' (Michael Coveney, *What's On Stage*). Where once its structure was questioned, it was now considered 'brilliant, radical and resonant' (Coveney). Critics were keen to point out the play's continued relevance in the twenty-first century, with Michael Billington (*Guardian*) branding it 'terrifyingly topical in its portrait of an individualistic society in which the few thrive at the expense of the many'. Several were also struck by how prescient Churchill's thirty-year-old play had been. Andrzej Lukowski (*Time Out*) suggested that with this play 'Churchill unerringly predicted the "culture of me" that has come to define our present' and that this revival 'suggests that "Top Girls" pinpoints the exact moment success overtook compassion as the cardinal social virtue' (Lyn Gardner was similarly awed by Churchill's prophetic ability in a *Guardian* article at the time of the 2002 production).

Other (mainly right-wing) journalists praised the play and production for its ability to document the period of economic and social change it depicts without resorting to didacticism. In the *Mail*, Patrick Marmion saw it as a story that 'doesn't take sides. Churchill merely observes the dying of one era and the mewling emergence of another'. And in the *Daily Telegraph*, Spencer concluded that whilst most 'plays about Thatcher's Britain were strident studies of social deprivation and blustering fury. In contrast *Top Girls* is oblique, witty, deeply felt and theatrically daring'. Whilst Churchill herself has been a fairly open critic of Thatcherism, the fact that these reviewers were able to make these assessments is testament to her play's dedication to providing debate rather than polemic.

The play is also a popular choice for amateur and educational productions, and is frequently performed in schools, colleges, universities and drama schools. In 2014, David Shirley directed a production with final year acting students at Manchester School of Theatre. He was interviewed by Sophie Bush on 3 February 2017.

SB: Why did you choose this play? What opportunities does it present for a young cast of actors?

DS: It enabled the young women to find a connection to a perspective on the world they would find interesting, especially in a post-Thatcherite world where many young women don't like to be seen to be too closely associated with feminism, particularly as young actresses. In the play you meet women from a wide spectrum of the past, but it points to the future as well, especially for young women about to enter what is still a male-dominated profession. Marlene's dilemma – wanting a career *and* to be a good mother – is one that many actresses are faced with today.

SB: And did it present any particular challenges?

DS: They found Act One hard, but they enjoyed the theatricality of it, so we made it about that – about storytelling, not politics. We just let these things sit beside each other and left it for the audience to make up their minds about what that meant. In this way, the cast were able to inhabit the play in their own womanhood. They weren't trying to play 'women from the past'.

SB: How did you go about ensuring you retained a sense of the play's original period, at the same time as ensuring it spoke to a contemporary audience?

DS: I never like doing a play entirely in its period. My production contained some modern resonances, such as mobile phones and a sound design which mixed and matched some 1980s tracks with more contemporary music, but if you're not careful, it looks like an attempt to 'rescue' an outdated play.

SB: Has the play 'dated' at all?

DS: On one level it does feel dated, because it speaks to a very particular moment in time, but these kinds of plays go through their datedness and get a new lease of life. It is certainly not dated if you are a young person discovering it fresh. Also, the play's central argument is very current. The central relationship between the sisters is particularly exciting. That quarrel has not gone away and is not dated.

Further reading

When considering the play in the context of the present day, think about which aspects of it strike you as being old-fashioned, no longer relevant or of their time, and which characters' concerns or experiences seem most significant to you. What do you consider to be the biggest issues facing women today? Or are you more concerned about issues that do not relate to gender?

Additionally, you could talk to your own families about the time period depicted in the play. Talk to your mothers, aunts and grandmothers about their perceptions of how women's roles within the family, society and the workplace have changed during their lifetimes, and their own approaches to managing family and/or career responsibilities.

All reviews quoted in this section are available in full online:

Billington, Michael (2011), Review of *Top Girls* at Chichester Festival Theatre. *Guardian* [online], 4 July. Available at: https://www.theguardian.com/stage/2011/jul/04/top-girls-review; accessed 16 April 2017.

Coveney, Michael (2011), Review of *Top Girls* at Trafalgar Studios. *What's On Stage* [online], 17 August. Available at: http://www.whatsonstage.com/west-end-theatre/reviews/08-2011/top-girls_7552.html; accessed 16 April 2017.

Gardner, Lyn (2002), 'Material girls'. *Guardian* [online], 2 January. Available at: https://www.theguardian.com/culture/2002/jan/02/ artsfeatures; accessed 16 April 2017.

Lukowski, Andrzej (2011), Review of *Top Girls* at Trafalgar Studios. *Time Out* [online], 22 August. Available at: https://www.timeout.com/ london/theatre/top-girls; accessed 16 April 2017.

Marmion, Patrick (2011), Review of *Top Girls* at Chichester Festival Theatre. *Mail* [online], 8 July. Available at: http://www.dailymail.co. uk/tvshowbiz/reviews/article-2012452/Top-Girls-review-A-giant-shoulder-pad-sized-slice-80s-girl-power.html; accessed 16 April 2017.

Spencer, Charles (2011), Review of *Top Girls* at Chichester Festival Theatre. *Telegraph* [online], 2 July. Available at: http://www.telegraph. co.uk/culture/theatre/theatre-reviews/8611489/Top-Girls-Minerva-Chichester-review.html; accessed 16 April 2017.

Themes

Women and work

The first act of the play sees Marlene celebrating her promotion to Managing Director of the Top Girls Employment Agency. Marlene's career – and to a certain extent the careers of her colleagues Nell and Win – do not seem to have been held back by sexist attitudes in the workplace. Nevertheless, such attitudes form a backdrop to the play, and are evident not just in the way men have behaved towards the women we meet, but in the women's own behaviour. The office scenes of the play all subtly contribute to an impression of a working world where it is still much easier for mediocre men to achieve than it is for above-average women to do so. When discussing a male client, whom they consider 'not overly bright', Win and Nell still see potential for a high-flying position for him, as long as 'his secretary can punctuate' (110). In other words, a skilled woman in a lowly paid, subordinate position will enable an inadequate man to succeed in a much better paid, senior position. Later we hear Louise recount a similar story: 'I've seen young men who I trained go on, in my own company, or elsewhere, to higher things' (120).

One of the play's most striking examples of male career entitlement is the scene in which Mrs Kidd (wife of an unseen colleague, Howard, who lost out on the promotion to Marlene) confronts Marlene. Mrs Kidd sees Marlene as 'not natural' and as 'one of those ballbreakers', who will 'end up miserable and lonely' (127), simply because Marlene will not submit to her idea that Howard is somehow more deserving of her job, and less able to accept the setback of not getting it 'because he's a man' (127). The moment where Marlene, who has hitherto been frostily polite with Mrs Kidd, loses her patience and finishes the conversation by asking Mrs Kidd 'Could you please piss off?' (128), is as delightful to an audience as it is to the watching Angie. However, elsewhere in the play, we see Marlene herself voice equally reductive attitudes towards women's role and potential in the workplace. For example, in her interview with Jeanine, Marlene warns her not to tell a potential employer that she is engaged to be married, particularly if she sends her for a job where the last girl 'left to have a baby' (117). This denial of motherhood, or even the potential for it, seems crucial to Marlene's conception of what it takes to succeed as a woman in work. In Act Three, she drunkenly and dreamily reminisces about a managing director she knows 'who's got two children, she breast feeds in the board room' (150), but her personal history of one abandoned child and two abortions suggests she does not put much faith in this ideal.

Alongside the rejection of motherhood, many of the women in the play allude to the necessity of renouncing other roles, traits or attributes that might be (mis)interpreted as feminine weaknesses in order to succeed in a 'man's world'. Nell has no interest in marrying – an action she sees as synonymous with 'play[ing] house' (112). Nell and Shona boast about not being very nice and never considering people's feelings, as an employer might worry that this tendency in women could reduce their effectiveness in sales (130). Win has abandoned a more altruistic career in medical research for the rather cynical reason that 'there's no money in it' (134); and Louise believes her modest career success comes as a result of her ability to 'pass as a man at work' (120), not literally in her dress or demeanour, but in terms of her credibility. Churchill's play does not explore alternative possibilities for women to be more authentically successful at work in terms they can define for themselves, but this absence highlights the need for such explorations, both in and out of the theatre.

The problems discussed in this section are associated with the privileged positions of the women presented in the agency scenes. At the other end of the social spectrum, we see the harsh reality of employment prospects for women like Angie and Joyce in a climate of rising unemployment, particularly outside London. This is discussed in more detail in the next section.

Mobility and stasis

Many of the women in the play fantasize about travel, movement and 'getting away'. Angie is transfixed by Marlene's account of driving across America in a fast car, and begs her to take her with her next time she goes (144). Both Marlene and Win have travelled extensively for their work. Shona dreams about 'burn[ing] up the M1 [. . .] in the fast lane' (131), and Jeanine hopes for a job opportunity which might allow her to travel (117). This concept of physical movement or mobility is strongly linked to the more abstract concept of social mobility: the ability to improve or change one's social status and opportunities. Marlene claims to have known, since she was thirteen, that her success and happiness depended on her ability to get away from her home and family: 'out of their house, out of them, never let that happen to me, [. . .] make my own way, out' (156). In physical terms, Marlene's movement has taken her from her rural community to London (as well as further afield); in social terms, it has 'raised' her from her working-class origins to the kind of high-flying executive lifestyle that funds the expensive dinner she hosts in Act One. By contrast, Joyce has made no movement at all, remaining within the same physical and class community into which she was born, and never expanding her prospects for herself or her family.

The play presents several factors that seem to contribute towards social mobility (or a lack thereof), one being access to/engagement with education. In Act Two, Scene One, Joyce wonders whether Angie should have stayed on at school, rather than leaving as soon as it was legally possible. When Kit reasons that Angie 'didn't like it', Joyce replies, 'I didn't like it. And look at me. If your face fits at school, it's going to fit other places too' (106). Educational success, cleverness and qualifications sit behind all the play's most successful women, regardless of their social origins, whilst those like Jeanine, who have few 'Os and As' (114), are given limited prospects, and those like Angie, who have none, are written off entirely.

Another factor is an individual's desire for change, which in Joyce seems quite limited. Joyce's strength and identity come from the certainties that have long been held within her family and community, most of which are connected to an 'us and them' mentality, which is highly suspicious of those who are better off, and is therefore unlikely to provoke self-advancement. However, whilst Churchill prompts us to question whether Joyce might have been able to achieve more, had she shared a little more of Marlene's self-determination and drive, this is carefully balanced by an equally important consideration of the effect of Joyce's personal and social circumstances. Where Marlene has been able to abandon all her familial responsibilities for the sake of her career, Joyce's keener sense of social and personal responsibility has prevented her from doing the same. Her willingness to take care of Angie and her aging mother has clearly limited her own ability to access further education or work, restricting her career opportunities to low-paid and insecure cleaning jobs.

Several critics point to Angie as the crucial force for positive movement or change within the play as, unlike Joyce, she is not prepared to continue the limited life she has been living but, unlike Marlene, she does not show such explicit disregard for her fellow women. However, Angie's potential for change remains tragically unrealized, as her birth mother (and society at large) is unwilling, and her adoptive mother (and community) unable, to help or support her to achieve her potential.

Female genealogy

The play's all female cast necessarily puts its focus on relationships between women. The following familial relationships (in both literal and metaphorical terms) are particularly important within the play.

Mothers

An obvious counterpoint to the theme of women and work is the prominent issue of potential mothers within the play not being able to raise children. All the women in the play's first act have either lost children through violence and coercion (Pope Joan is stoned to death moments after the birth of her child, who she presumes has also been killed; Gret has lost children to war; Nijo has had to give up the children born to her lovers, so as not to lose the Emperor's favour; and Griselda has had to give up hers to placate the strange whims of her husband), or by foregoing their child-bearing potential, as in the case of Isabella. Marlene's voluntary abandonment of Angie might seem all the more callous alongside some of these women's tragic losses, but Marlene too can be seen to have been coerced into her decision not to raise her own child, albeit by (lack of) social opportunity rather than direct violence or threat.

Daughters

The play makes many references to the lack of value ascribed to, and potential for, girl children. This is most clearly voiced by Nijo. As Griselda relates her story of having her first child taken away, Nijo asks, 'Was it a boy?' When Griselda tells her it was a girl, Nijo consoles, 'Even so, it's hard when they take it away' (87). When Griselda explains that she later had a boy, Nijo responds, 'Ah a boy. So it all ended happily' (88). When recounting her own story of lost children, Nijo says of one child, 'It was only a girl but I was sorry to lose it' (80).

Whilst Nijo's attitudes are intended to be representative of a past age, even in the modern world of the play Angie faces a future lacking in opportunity for girls with her socio-economic background. Joyce is blunt about this, expressing that 'She'd better get married', as 'She's not going to get a job when jobs are hard to get' (106). Marlene also sees the limit of Angie's opportunities as being a "Packer in Tesco' (135). The last thing Marlene says about Angie, chronologically speaking, is that 'She's not going to make it' (135).

Angie has been abandoned by Marlene to a life of few prospects, but this lack of care on a personal level is mirrored by a much more general sense that the world of the play is not adequately protecting or providing opportunity for its (girl) children. In Act Two, Scene One, this is evident in Kit's anxiety over the threat of 'the war' (101) and its weaponry that can see 'Your skin's burned right off' (100). Kit seeks to protect herself by becoming a nuclear physicist (106), going to New Zealand (100), or standing in the bomb's epicentre to ensure instant annihilation rather than a slow painful death, 'walking round with your skin dragging on the ground' (101).

It is perhaps unsurprising, given the treatment of children within the play, that some of them have become angry. In Act Two, Scene One, Angie expresses the desire to kill her mother whilst Kit watches. This gives her threat an almost ritualistic quality, which is re-emphasized at the end of the scene when Angie returns to the stage, having specially put on the dress that Marlene gave her a year earlier, telling Kit: 'I put on this dress to kill my mother' (108).

Sisters

Though Isabella is the only woman in the play's first act to have not given up her own child, she does discuss the loss of her sister Hennie (who she often refers to as one might a child or even a 'pet'), whose company she gives up for the sake of her travels and who later dies. Hennie, in some ways, serves for Isabella the same function Joyce serves for Marlene. By waiting at home, fulfilling the expectations of her gender, Hennie gives purpose and meaning to Isabella's travels, and a sense of somewhere to return to. Likewise, Marlene's adventures are possible only because Joyce has stayed at home to care for her daughter and their aging parents. Isabella's comment that Hennie's death made her feel like 'half of myself had gone' (75) underlines the crucial function these women play in the lives of their more active sisters.

'We won't wait': a disregard for sisterhood

In the first line of the play, Marlene tells the waitress that one of their party is 'going to be late but we won't wait' (63). This might read like a throwaway comment, but it encapsulates something of her attitude towards all of the other women in the play: they are only welcome, or valued, as long as they are not holding her up. When the other women toast her success, she includes them in it, but this seems a somewhat token gesture set against the more material reality of her actions. Marlene is not alone in her disregard for other women in this act, as is evident in several of her guests' attitudes to class. When Isabella condemns the barbaric behaviour amongst the lower classes in the East, Nijo does not bother to defend them, claiming simply that she 'wouldn't know' about their behaviour (70).

Marlene shows equal disregard for the women in the play's second half. She ignores her sister and daughter for long periods of time, returning to them with expensive luxury gifts that are of no practical value. She thus gives them charity rather than support, and Joyce's realization of this is evident in her refusal of Marlene's

money and ingratitude for her gifts. Marlene's colleagues tell us
'She never talks about her family' (134), further underscoring her
disregard for these women.

In the office scenes, Win and Nell discuss the lack of potential for
them to be promoted within their company now 'Marlene's filled [. . .]
up' all the room at the top (110). In her interview with Jeanine,
Marlene dampens the young woman's ambitions to work in
advertising and to travel with work, using a mixture of stereotypical
assumptions about women – 'Does your fiancé want to travel?',
'You'll have children' (117) – and discouraging statements about
Jeanine's lack of skills and experience. Marlene is not overtly cruel
or unhelpful; she finds some jobs that, whilst not as glamorous as
Jeanine is hoping for, are reasonable prospects for her, and in fact
closes the interview with an encouraging statement of belief in
Jeanine's abilities. However, her dismissive attitude and failure to
really listen to what Jeanine is trying to tell her demonstrate her lack
of genuine commitment to helping other women succeed.

There is also an ageism or generational tension within the play.
Win is frank with Louise that her middle age is 'a handicap' (118)
that is unlikely to be off-set by the advantage her added experience
brings. (In a previous scene, she has been equally dismissive towards
the mention of a male client of a similar age.) Louise, in turn, is
suspicious of a new 'kind of woman who is thirty now who grew up
in a different climate. They are not so careful. They take themselves
for granted'. Louise sees that these new women have made an asset
out of being 'attractive' and 'well-dressed', in comparison to her own
approach of aspiring to 'pass as a man' (120). Jozefina Komporaly
sees this conflict echoed by the play's first act, in which some
'women, like Isabella or Pope Joan, reached fame by assuming roles
so far reserved for men', whilst 'others, like Nijo or Griselda, did
so by emphasizing their archetypal feminine qualities, and by
encouraging conformity to male expectations' (2006: 51).

Fathers

Whilst no men, and therefore no fathers, are physically present
within this play, the shadows of fathers (and the 'patriarchy' more
generally) hang heavily over it. Isabella has tried and failed to please

her clergyman father; Nijo's father allows her to be given to the Emperor as his concubine; and Griselda's father is the one who is first consulted about her marriage to the Marquis. In the modern world, Marlene's and Joyce's abusive father haunts their relationship, causing them to argue over whether his violence towards their mother was simply his own unforgivable fault, or a symptom of his hard and limited life (155–6).

'Herstory'

The play's first act shows Marlene choosing to celebrate her success, not with her family, or even her real-life friends (if she has any) or colleagues, but with a group of fictional, historical and mythical women. In doing so, she signals her affinity to an alternative genealogy of women. She rejects the ties of blood relationships and situates herself against a backdrop of significant and notable women, many of whom have nonetheless received little historical or critical attention. Crucially, Churchill does not choose the most famous women from history, legend or literature to people this scene: no Queen Elizabeth I or Victoria, Boudicca, Lady Macbeth or Cleopatra. She chooses women who have been all but forgotten to those without a specialist interest in their stories. In doing so, she participates in a feminist practice known as 'herstory': the reclamation of important but largely forgotten women and assertion that their stories are as important as the figures that fill the pages of traditional, male-authored *his*tory books. The term 'herstory' was coined by feminist scholar Robin Morgan in her 1970 anthology *Sisterhood is Powerful*. As well as researching into the backgrounds and stories of the women presented in Act One, you might consider which six women from history, fiction or legend you would invite, if you were having your own dinner party, and why you would want them to be there.

Celebration or critique?

A central question raised by the play is the extent to which the success of women like Marlene is to be celebrated or its limitations critiqued. Churchill's questioning attitude to this dilemma is evident in her multiple revisions of the play's title (recounted in Roberts 2008: 81). Early drafts considered *Successful Women* and *Heroines*, but Churchill explains: 'I was afraid that one wouldn't see the irony of the title. Perhaps people don't see the irony of calling it *Top Girls*'. Churchill's own irony towards this title signals a critique of Marlene's success, which is underscored by her decision to structure the second act as 'Angie's story', making it impossible to view the 'office scenes as a celebration of Marlene, the achiever' (Aston 2010: 41). However, she was keen that the play should not present a one-sided argument about any of the dilemmas its characters confront:

> I did want people to feel that Marlene was wrong, I suppose, in rejecting Angie [. . .]. But I think it's complicated and prevented from being just a simple black and white thing by the fact that Marlene has all the attractive qualities of wanting adventure and change even though it's actually . . . a goal that ultimately I suspect, I hope, the audience wouldn't agree with. And equally that Joyce, through having other views that I would share is also in some ways rather limited and bad tempered so that it wasn't just a case of pitching a good person and a bad person.
>
> (Churchill cited in Roberts 2008: 86)

Churchill was also keen to stress the celebratory nature of the play's first act, which she intended as a 'festive scene', with conversation mainly 'at the level of amusing anecdotes, of sharing stories and entertaining each other'. She has criticized a German production of the play which presented the first act characters as 'miserable and quarrelsome and competitive' (cited in Roberts 2008: 211). The academic Geraldine Cousin also considers that 'overwhelmingly, the first scene is a celebration' (1989: 95). Nevertheless, these claims can seem difficult to reconcile with the stage directions at the end of the scene, which see Nijo crying, Joan vomiting and Marlene drinking heavily (94), and it does not seem unreasonable that the scholar Janelle Reinelt assesses that, despite their considerable achievements, Marlene's dinner guests 'had not been happy' (in Aston and Reinelt 2000: 180). However, when you read or watch the first scene with foreknowledge of the darker conclusion of the play, it can be particularly difficult not to filter it through this knowledge, so it is important to remember that if you were viewing it for the first time, it would be easier to be caught up by its exciting, theatrical atmosphere. For Churchill, this scene was intended to present Marlene as 'a sort of feminist heroine who had done things against extraordinary odds, so that we could then have a different attitude to her as the play went on and we could begin to question what her values actually were' (cited in Roberts 2008: 214).

Dramatic Devices

Language

Overlapping dialogue

Whilst *Top Girls* is sometimes credited with the theatrical invention of overlapping dialogue, Aston (2010: 39), Roberts (2008: 80) and Cousin (1989: 101) all point to Churchill's previous experimentation with a similar but slightly simpler technique in her much less well-known play *Three More Sleepless Nights* (Soho Poly, 1980). However, there is no doubt that *Top Girls* brought this device to a wider audience, particularly as its original production published the play text as a programme, giving critics and audiences a direct insight into Churchill's method of scoring dialogue to indicate where speakers overlap and talk over one another, using the following punctuation key:

- A forward slash (/) indicates the point at which a character is interrupted by the next speaker. This may be a short interjection, or the other character may continue at length over the first speaker.
- An asterisk (*) at the end of a line indicates that this line cues not only the one that immediately follows it (as in conventional dramatic layout), but another as well.
- An asterisk (*) at the beginning of a line indicates that this line also follows the last line that ended with an asterisk.

A number of interpretations have been offered for this dramatic technique. The most obvious explanation for it might be that it enables Churchill to create dialogue that more closely resembles the way people speak in real life. In every day, informal conversations, people do not often wait their turn to speak, but interject as and when they feel compelled to respond to a particular point. Some interruptions signal rudeness or disrespect for others' speech, whilst some are a natural result of the ebb and flow of conversation and may signal support, encouragement or excitement, rather than disrespect, towards another's speech. Philip Roberts sees the technique as one primarily designed to enhance naturalism, suggesting that 'the layering and intercutting of what is said produces precisely the effect of a normal dinner party'. However, he also suggests that it contributes to a thematic effect as the layered speech produces 'composites, as well as individuals' so that a more general pattern of 'women's experience is formulated, as well as individual lives' (2008: 83). Geraldine Cousin reads the device in a similar way, suggesting that the 'stories overlap and interweave, so that one anecdote merges into, and enriches the pattern of the rest' (1989: 95).

Other critics suggest the linguistic model displayed here is less positive. Elaine Aston sees it as evidence that 'the women are largely and self-centredly caught up in their own individual narratives'. She interprets their overlapping dialogue as Churchill's underscoring of their 'inability to listen to and to share experiences with women [. . .] indicative of intrasexual oppression' (2010: 39). Janelle Reinelt also concludes that the play presents Marlene's dinner guests as 'self-centred and unable to communicate well with others', through the 'theatrical technique of overlapping speeches so that the women talk on top of each other' (in Aston and Reinelt 2000: 180). Theatre critic Benedict Nightingale changed his interpretation over the course of watching the first production, describing

> a device I first thought was supposed to add realism to Max Stafford-Clark's finely played production, but later suspected was meant to imply some lack of mutual attention. Women don't listen to each other enough, don't learn sufficiently from their accumulated experience.

If at all possible, do try to read the play aloud in a group, so you can hear and experiment with this technique in practice.

Voice

All the women in the play have very distinct voices. One of the most notable differences between them is the amount of time/words allocated to each speaker, as well as the ways in which they use language. In the play's first act, this ranges from the entirely silent waitress, through the blunt, monosyllabic Gret, to the brusque Isabella, poetic Nijo and erudite Joan, who is want to talk obliquely of theological theories and quote large sections of Latin. Not only do these women have distinct linguistic differences, they also disagree about what some words mean, due to their differing historical and social backgrounds. For example, Marlene expresses concern at Nijo's rape by the Emperor as a teenage courtesan, but Nijo sees the experience not as rape but as a necessary rite of passage into her intended courtly life. However, it is Gret's language, or lack of it, which sets her most clearly apart from the other women, and this is fundamentally connected to her lower social or class status.

The connection between language and class is carried forward into the rest of the play. In Act Two, Scene One, this is less obvious, because Kit, Angie and Joyce share a similar background. Even so, Joyce's speech is likely to appear a little coarse to audiences, perhaps even shockingly or comically so, as when she shouts from offstage and calls Angie a 'fucking rotten little cunt' (100). Kit and Angie's dialogue in this scene contains lots of short lines, often of only a few words each, giving their speech an appropriately childish quality of quick retorts and sudden changes of subject. The two girls are relatively well matched in their ability to communicate with one another throughout most of the scene, but when Angie tries to exert power over Kit through commanding language, she is outsmarted by Kit's better logic:

Angie   What if I left you here in the dark all night?

Kit   You couldn't. I'd go home. (97)

However, we do not fully appreciate the limitations of Angie's linguistic experience until we hear her in the new environment of Marlene's office. When Mrs Kidd attempts the formal greeting 'Very pleased to meet you', Angie answers with a non-sequitur, 'Very well thank you' (126). Similarly, when Win tries to joke with her, 'Who's been eating my porridge?', Angie is completely nonplussed by this playful use of language and metaphor. Likewise, when Win asks the rhetorical question 'How did you guess?', Angie gives a genuine and considered answer: 'Because you look as if you might work here and you're sitting at the desk' (132–3).

It is important to understand that Angie's simple use of language and misunderstanding of more complex linguistic models does not signal a lack of intelligence, rather a more limited set of references through which to understand the world. Marlene, Joyce and Angie all come from the same socio-economic, or class, background, but Marlene has benefited from the concept of social mobility in a way that Angie and Joyce have not. Consequently, Marlene's frames of reference and expectation, as evidenced through her language, are very different to Angie's and Joyce's. When Angie arrives in Marlene's office, Marlene cannot understand why she would rather be there than out shopping or visiting popular tourist attractions like the Tower of London and Madame Tussauds (122): activities that would never have occurred to Angie, who has never travelled far from her home or been in the privileged position of being a 'tourist' (a concept that is also clearly alien to Joyce, who in Act Three disparagingly describes 'strangers walking' near their home 'on a Sunday' (146)). One of the starkest examples of Marlene's and Angie's different frames of reference is when the two remember the day, a year earlier, that Marlene visited Joyce and Angie (the scene that takes place in Act Three). 'Yes, that was nice wasn't it?' says Marlene, blandly. 'That was the best day of my whole life', enthuses Angie (124–5). Similarly, when Marlene questions Angie's desire to sit and wait for her in the office, rather than go sightseeing and come back, Angie professes that the office is 'where I most want to be in the world' (128).

Marlene's movement away from her upbringing, both ideologically and linguistically, is equally apparent throughout her confrontations with Joyce in Act Three. For example, Joyce's speech includes dialect phrases that are not grammatically correct in Standard English ('if you wasn't going to keep it. You was the most stupid' (150)), whereas Marlene's speech does not. Though Marlene has clearly refined her speech in line with her new lifestyle, her class roots remain evident in certain words and phrases she uses, such as calling people 'pet'.

Structure

The play has an ambiguous, partially non-linear, or non-chronological, structure. The first scene takes place in a fantasy setting, which sits outside 'real' time, as we understand it. This enables women from a wide range of historical periods and from fiction and legend to meet to discuss their common concerns, as well as their considerable differences. Many themes that are established in this scene link it to the rest of the play, and in most productions the actors who perform the historical women reappear to play other characters in Acts Two and Three. However, because Marlene is the only character from the first act who is carried forward as the narrative unfolds into the play's second and third acts, Act One can appear to stand alone or stand out from the rest of the play, a device that both baffled and excited critics of the first production. Additionally, because Marlene does not appear, and is not even named when Angie discusses her aunt in Act Two, Scene One, this scene initially appears to bear no relation to Act One. Until Angie arrives at Marlene's office in the next scene, an audience or reader will not understand how Act Two, Scene One is linked to the dinner party scene, or to the initial part of the scene at the Top Girls agency. However, Act Two is, in other ways, far more conventional in its dramatic structure, progressing in chronological order and probably covering just two days of real time (though the text does not specify this time span, this was Max Stafford-Clark's interpretation; see interview). The final moment of this act, where Marlene pronounces that Angie is 'not going to make it' (135), is the last thing we see in terms of the play's chronology.

The third act of the play makes the only directly non-chronological shift in its structure, taking us back in time a year. It is important to remember that the visit that Marlene makes to Angie and Joyce in this scene, and the argument the sisters have, which may be at least partially overheard by Angie, has happened before the events of Act Two, and subsequently informs the behaviour of these women in the back yard and office scenes.

As we have seen in the discussion of the play's initial critical response, its unusual structure proved exciting to some, but off-putting to many. Even Max Stafford-Clark was initially concerned about the extent of the play's structural innovations, writing in his diary upon receiving the play: 'Structure difficult – where to make the act changes. Fuck. How do we know it's a year earlier?' (cited in Roberts 2008: 209). However, he soon came to recognize the opportunities this lack of linearity presented, explaining, 'it is midway through the second act before the exposition is over [. . .]: you're titillating the audience by withholding information' (cited in Roberts 2008: 213). Today, such challenges to the traditional structure of the 'well-made play' are far more frequently employed by writers and accepted and appreciated by audiences.

The play's three-act structure, as published in this edition, is Churchill's preferred mode of presentation. However, due to the practicalities of staging a play with two intervals, the initial production was presented in two acts, with the interval after the scene set in Angie's back yard. This (along with some alterations to the structure of Act Two, made to allow for the practicalities of actors playing more than one role to change costume) has led to some discrepancies between previous publications of the text (and consequently to the way it is discussed in some academic sources). Clearly, such practical considerations have a real and important effect on the staging and reception of work written for the live, collaborative medium of theatre, and must be weighed against the importance of the playwright's intentions for their work. Whilst Churchill has been flexible enough to make compromises with those staging her play, it is important to consider her intended structure and her reasons for it. In this case, these are particularly interesting, as Churchill's preference for the three-act structure is intended to foreground the second act as 'Angie's story' (cited in Aston 2010: 41): an interesting repositioning of subjectivity within the play, which challenges the tendency to view Marlene alone as its central character.

Characterization

The play contains sixteen characters, twelve of which appear in only one scene of the play (and Kit only appears for seconds outside her main scene). Marlene, Joyce and Angie are the only characters we are able to observe in more than one time or place, and even they are not observed to 'develop' in traditional dramatic terms, as we in fact witness them move backwards in time between Acts Two and Three. Evidently, the play is not therefore focused on character development, but on presenting a mosaic or patchwork of varied and contrasting characters, in order to build up a picture of women's experience through 'collage' rather than narrative progression. This said, each character presented, however briefly, is psychologically developed, in line with a realist tradition of playwriting. They may contain some symbolic or representative characteristics, or voice particular lines of argument, but they are not simply cyphers or mouthpieces to convey Churchill's underlying meaning. Rather, they are recognizable women and challenging and rewarding roles.

All-female cast

Given the number of plays with an all-male cast, it may seem odd to class this as a notable or significant dramatic technique. However, Churchill's use of an all-female cast was both deliberate and unusual for a mainstream theatre piece at the time of its initial production (though more common within the work of feminist collectives such as the Women's Theatre Group). For Churchill, 'the idea was to offer a huge range of different parts and give women the opportunity to play lots of roles on stage which they don't always get to play' (cited in Roberts 2008: 211–12). Janelle Reinelt picks up on this aspect of the play in her chapter in *The Cambridge Companion to Caryl Churchill*, commenting on the importance of 'the range of female types' depicted, particularly in the middle act of the play. For Reinelt, this mosaic of women of varying ages, backgrounds and outlooks helps Churchill 'chart the difficulty of women bonding with each other in a competitive economic climate' (Reinelt in Aston and Diamond 2009: 30–1).

Multi-roling

In her previous play *Cloud Nine*, Churchill had used multi-roling (whereby each actor plays more than one character within the play), alongside deliberately casting against race and gender, as a form of comment on the characters' ingrained beliefs and prejudices. Thus, Betty, the play's central female character, is played by a man in the first half of the play, as her performance of womanhood has been entirely constructed by men. In *Top Girls*, the doubling that is usually employed to stage the play has more to do with economics than aesthetics. Max Stafford-Clark recounts his initial dismay at receiving a play with sixteen characters, as he knew he would not be able to afford to stage it, until he and Churchill worked out a minimum cast of seven could be achieved by doubling and trebling certain roles.

Although initially a matter of expediency, there is undoubtedly a certain effect produced by seeing the women from the play's first act repopulate the stage in more contemporary guises throughout Acts Two and Three. In particular, Stafford-Clark points to the resonance achieved by casting the same actress in the roles of Dull Gret and Angie: arguably the play's two most socially disadvantaged characters, shown the least regard by Marlene. For academic Dan Rebellato, this achieved a profound effect where 'the first character seemed to hang ghostlike in the presence of the second, and the vision of hell conjured by Gret carried forward and underscored Angie's own journey into nightmare' (cited in Aston 2010: 124). Even where there are less obvious parallels between the two (or sometimes three) characters played by each actress, Jozefina Komporaly suggests that the use of multi-roling implies the 'interconnectedness of women's experience' (2006: 50); and Elaine Aston has suggested that Marlene's 'identification with dominant, masculine values is reflected in the way in which actress and role are constant, unlike the "unfixing" strategies encoded in the doubling of other characters' (2010: 40). When considering this aspect of the play, think about how you would cast it, if you were directing a production. Which roles, if any, would you double, and why?

Theatrical style

The restaurant setting and consumption of the dinner is vital to the theatricality and tone of the play's opening act. As recognized by both Max Stafford-Clark and David Shirley in their directorial processes, the material reality of this staging provides a much-needed anchor to ground the abstract and philosophical scene for its actors and give them a more tangible approach. Staging the scene requires a huge logistical undertaking as real food must be ordered, prepared, served, consumed and cleared away with precision timing, as this process coincides with certain lines in the dialogue, throughout the scene. The influence of a Brechtian, material or social realism is noticeable here: what each woman chooses to eat and how she consumes her food is rooted in her social position and experience. This is nowhere more noticeable than in Gret's desire for nothing more than bread and potatoes.

The third act of *Top Girls*, with its domestic setting in the kitchen of Joyce's working-class home, is reminiscent of a type of theatre termed from the late 1950s as 'kitchen sink' realism, and was described as such in reviews of the original production (Warden, Satchell). Plays recognized as part of this movement away from the 'drawing room' settings prevalent amongst pre- and post-war writing from playwrights such as Terence Rattigan, Noël Coward, Oscar Wilde and J.B. Priestley, include John Osborne's *Look Back in Anger* (often heralded as the start of this movement), Shelagh Delaney's *A Taste of Honey*, and Edward Bond's *Saved*. The gritty realism associated with this movement of drama is, however, undercut in Churchill's play by her break with linear time structures, and inclusion of an overtly theatrical first act.

Whilst the consumption of real food gives the play's first scene a level of realism, which the audience may be able to smell, as well as see, depending on the intimacy of the performance venue, this act is also imbued with elements of fantasy and spectacle. For Max Stafford-Clark, this was intensified by staging the play in a way that allowed the entrance of each new character to be highly signalled to, and enjoyed by, the audience. Philip Roberts discusses this effect:

> In the original production of 1982, the glass front of the restaurant formed the set's back wall. The restaurant entrance was upstage right. The parade of historical figures all entered upstage left and walked the full width of the stage before entering. Thus, they could be seen before they entered and spoke. The effect was equivalent to a 'whodunit' or, rather, a 'who-is-it?' The audience, held in suspense, waited for the figures to arrive.

(2008: 82–3)

Clearly, the unusual and varied costumes required by the characters in this scene, due to their range of social, historical and geographical origins, adds to its sense of spectacle, as you can see by searching online for production photographs or images from costume designers' portfolios.

Further Study

University students should find a good range of the following texts available in their institutional libraries. School and college libraries may stock a more limited range of materials, but if you live near a university, you should be able to sign in and access their library as a visitor. You may not be able to take books out, but you can access their collections and there will be places you can sit and read with your notebook or laptop.

Academic debate

Adiseshiah, Sian (2009), *Churchill's Socialism: Political Resistance in the Plays of Caryl Churchill*. Newcastle: Cambridge Scholars Publishing.

This book provides an interesting counterpoint to much of the scholarship on Churchill's work, which tends to consider it predominantly from a feminist angle. Its fourth chapter (pp. 133–64) considers class and gender in *Top Girls*, alongside Churchill's next play, *Fen* (1983), exploring the interplay and tensions between socialism and feminism presented within these two contrasting works. The book's opening chapter also provides a helpful insight into the political, social and cultural contexts in which Churchill was writing.

Aston, Elaine (2003), *Feminist Views on the English Stage: Women Playwrights, 1990–2000*. Cambridge: Cambridge University Press.

Elaine Aston is one of the foremost scholars of Churchill's work and feminist and women's theatre practice more generally. This book's second chapter ('Telling feminist tales: Caryl Churchill', pp. 18–36) focusses on Churchill and highlights her continued significance. 'Churchill's theatre', stresses Aston, 'has been enormously important to the subsequent generations of playwrights (men and women) and to the evolution of a contemporary feminist theatre practice' (18). This chapter, like Komporaly's book (see below), focusses on the mother–child relationships in Churchill's work, considering *Top Girls* alongside two more recent plays: *The Skriker* (1994) and *Blue Heart* (1997).

Aston, Elaine (2010), *Caryl Churchill*. Third Edition. Tavistock: Northcote House Publishers.

This book will appeal to more advanced academic readers. It includes a developed discussion of *Top Girls* (pp. 38–45), which highlights themes such as 'inter- and intra-sexual oppression' (the oppression of women by men, and by each other) and the importance of 'geographical mobility' to the varying independence of the women in the play. Aston writes from an explicitly feminist perspective, discussing Churchill's work within the context of feminist theatre practice, and highlighting its effect on the female spectator in particular.

Aston, Elaine and Elin Diamond (eds) (2009), *The Cambridge Companion to Caryl Churchill*. Cambridge: Cambridge University Press.

More advanced readers might also like to consider the variously authored essays in this edited collection. This book is trickier to navigate than some of the others discussed here, as its chapters discuss Churchill's work thematically, rather than chronologically, but there is an extended discussion of *Top Girls* in Janelle Reinelt's chapter 'On feminist and sexual politics' (pp. 30–2), and several other contributors reference the play in relation to the other texts on which they focus. Dan Rebellato's final chapter, which charts Churchill's influences as well as her considerable influence on contemporary theatre, is particularly helpful in contextualizing her whole body of work.

Aston, Elaine and Janelle Reinelt (2000), *The Cambridge Companion to Modern British Women Playwrights*. Cambridge: Cambridge University Press.

This edited collection also contains a chapter on Churchill by Janelle Reinelt (pp. 174–93), which includes discussion of *Top Girls*. This chapter is included within a section of the book called 'The question of canon', which contains two other chapters on Pam Gems and

Sarah Daniels, respectively. Placing Churchill's work within this context demonstrates its centrality within the study of contemporary women playwrights, and suggests its influence. Reinelt begins her chapter by proposing that Churchill is 'arguably the most successful and best-known socialist-feminist playwright to have emerged from Second Wave feminism' (174).

Cousin, Geraldine (1989), *Churchill: The Playwright*. London: Methuen Drama.

Cousin discusses Churchill's broader body of work (though only, of course, up until 1989 when her book was published). Her section on *Top Girls* is quite short, predominately focussed on the play's narrative, and discusses an earlier publication of the play text, which has a slightly different act structure. It is also clear that this book was published before *Top Girls* had become recognized as quite the seminal work it is today. However, the book's overall conclusion, which highlights some recurrent themes and concerns within Churchill's work (such as the 'necessity of change' (123), the effects of the political on the personal, and the importance of children), as well as her experimentation with temporal structure and use of 'vivid and haunting' visual imagery (126), may also be of interest to students of this play.

Gobert, R. Darren (2014), *The Theatre of Caryl Churchill*. London: Bloomsbury.

A well-developed section on *Top Girls* can be found in this book, which is particularly useful for its discussion of the contexts around the play's original and subsequent productions, and the role played by Max Stafford-Clark in its devolvement. Published in 2014, the book is also able to situate the play within its contemporary context, highlighting its central importance within Churchill's career, as well as discussing how her work has developed into the twenty-first century.

Komporaly, Jozefina (2006), *Staging Motherhood: British Women Playwrights, 1956 to the Present*. Basingstoke: Palgrave Macmillan.

This book's second chapter ('Irreversible choice: female professional success', pp. 34–58) contains a section on *Top Girls* (pp. 49–56) which focusses, as the title of the volume suggests, on the representation of motherhood in the play. Komporaly compares the character of Marlene to the character of Marion in Churchill's earlier stage play, *Owners* (Royal Court, 1972), and also draws parallels to Pam Gems's 1977 play *Queen Christina*, discussing each character's adoption of traditionally masculine and/or feminine values and attributes.

Kritzer, Amelia Howe (1991), *The Plays of Caryl Churchill*. Basingstoke: Macmillan.

This book contains a particularly useful chapter entitled 'Labour and capital' (pp. 138–71), a subsection of which (pp. 138–50) focusses on *Top Girls*. Kritzer examines the play's conflicting themes of 'competition' and 'care', highlighting the difficult position of women, who must choose either between the equally unsavoury options of continuing in poorly or non-paid roles as carers, or abandoning care for others to succeed alongside men in a competitive, capitalist world; or find some alternative route, not depicted within Churchill's play, but so clearly signalled as needed.

Luckhurst, Mary (2015), *Caryl Churchill*. London and New York: Routledge.

The most recent volume to focus specifically on Churchill's work, this book is up-to-date, informative and accessible. It contains an extensive chapter on *Top Girls* (pp. 83–105), much of which is focused on differing attitudes towards the characters of Marlene, Joyce and Angie between the original production and more contemporary revivals. Luckhurst also draws attention to the important issue of critics over-emphasizing the significance of the play, to the exclusion of work by other female playwrights, and of using Churchill (and specifically this play) as *the* example of feminist or women's playwriting, rather than considering the full depth and breadth of this field.

Roberts, Philip (2008), *About Churchill: The Playwright and the Work*. London: Faber and Faber.

A very useful account of Churchill's work, particularly because of the wealth of previously unpublished documentary, archival and interview material it discusses. These sources offer revealing insights into the production and reception of Churchill's plays, from the perspectives of actors, directors and, of course, Churchill herself. The book contains two extended sections on *Top Girls* (pp. 81–8 and pp. 208–18), though, like Cousin's book, it discusses a slightly different edition of the play text. Roberts's description of Angie as a character who 'has special needs' is also somewhat problematic, especially as he then goes on to quote Lesley Sharp, who played the character, asserting Angie's brightness (216–17).

Tyler, Alicia (2008), *Caryl Churchill's Top Girls*. **London and New York: Continuum.**

Alicia Tyler has written an accessible study guide to the play, which gives a detailed account of Churchill's biographical and professional background, an extensive commentary on the play text and a discussion of its production history in the UK and abroad. It also includes a selection of exercises and discussion points for students and teachers of the play to use in class workshops, or to guide individual reflection.

Academic journals

As well as full-length books, many academics have written shorter journal articles about *Top Girls* and Churchill's work more broadly. These may be more difficult for school and college students to get hold of, but again, universities should have access to many. You can search for journal articles directly through your university library's catalogue, or through subject-specific databases such as the International Index to Performing Arts (IIPA), JSTOR or the MLA International Bibliography, which allow you to use key terms (such as 'Caryl Churchill Top Girls') to find materials relevant to your studies. If you are uncertain about how to access such resources, ask a librarian or tutor for further guidance.

Comparative literature

Other work by Churchill

Churchill's output is huge, spanning every decade from the 1960s to the present day. Her works are published in four volumes of collected full-length plays and a volume of 'Shorts', as well as in multiple single publications. Any are worth reading, but below is a small selection that might resonate particularly with the study of *Top Girls*.

Owners (1972)

Published in: Churchill, Caryl (1985), *Plays: 1*. London: Methuen.

This play was Churchill's first professionally staged production, opening at the Royal Court in 1972, and beginning her long association with that theatre. The play is seen by many as a precursor to *Top Girls*, as it explores some similar themes, such as the ruthlessness of capitalist ideology. Its focus is on the concept of ownership, of both property and human beings. Whilst the former is depicted through a narrative of house-buying and property development, the latter is explored through the toxic and abusive relationships of the play's five central characters. One of these, Marion, a successful but morally bankrupt businesswoman, bears some comparison to Marlene. Marion's disregard for sisterhood is evident in her opinion that: 'Most women are fleas but I'm the dog' (30). However, the character and the play in general are altogether crueller and bleaker than *Top Girls*.

Cloud Nine (1979)

Published in: Churchill, Caryl (1985), *Plays: 1*. London: Methuen.

Developed shortly before *Top Girls*, this play sees Churchill experiment with a non-literal approach to temporal structure, which she would return to in order to produce the impossible dinner party that opens the later play. *Cloud Nine* has two acts set over a century apart. The first takes place in a British colony in nineteenth-century Africa; the second in London in 1979 (the year the play was written). However, both acts feature several of the same characters, who have aged just twenty-five years over this time. This device allowed Churchill, and the Joint Stock Company led by Max Stafford-Clark (with whom she developed the play through workshops), to explore the shifts and stagnation in attitudes towards gender and sexual politics over this period.

Far Away (2000)

Published in: Churchill, Caryl (2008), *Plays: 4*. London: Nick Hern Books.

In the opening scene of *Far Away*, a little girl comes downstairs after she has been put to bed to recount to her aunt the frightening noises and sights that have woken her. What we first mistake for a child's sleepy imaginings are gradually and chillingly revealed to be the sinister reality of her aunt and uncle's life. There are resonances here with the final moments of *Top Girls*, when Angie wakes to confront the 'frightening' realities of her world. Both plays highlight the way in which adults have failed to protect their world's children.

Work by other writers

Again, this is only a small sample of plays it would be interesting to consider alongside *Top Girls*. You could also look at any of the other plays that have been mentioned throughout this commentary.

A Taste of Honey (1958)

Published as: Delaney, Shelagh (2014), *A Taste of Honey*. London: Methuen Drama.

Shelagh Delaney's first play, *A Taste of Honey*, shares some thematic concerns with Churchill's work. The two women at the centre of Delaney's play are Helen and Jo, a troubled mother and daughter, as socially disadvantaged as Joyce and Angie. Delaney demonstrates how difficult it is to be a 'good mother' under the circumstances in which Helen and Jo live, despite Jo's determination not to repeat her mother's inadequacies when she falls pregnant herself.

New Anatomies (1981) and *The Grace of Mary Traverse* (1985)

Published in: Wertenbaker, Timberlake (1996), *Plays: 1*. London: Faber and Faber.

Written for the feminist collective the Women's Theatre Group, *New Anatomies* looks at the issue of women having to assume male characteristics, behaviour and dress in order to access the same successes and adventures available to men. Similarly to the depiction of real historical figures, such as Isabella Bird and Lady Nijo, in the first act of *Top Girls*, *New Anatomies* takes as its central character the nineteenth-century woman Isabelle Eberhardt, who spent most of her adult life dressed as an Arab man, in order to travel regions of the Sahara that were inaccessible to European women.

Produced by the Royal Court, where Wertenbaker was, as Churchill had been, Writer in Residence, *The Grace of Mary Traverse* features a central character who, like Marlene, owes something of her creation to Margaret Thatcher's rise to power. Like Thatcher and Marlene, Mary has a ruthless, individualistic outlook on her world (which in Mary's case is eighteenth-century London), and shows little concern for the weaker souls she tramples on her way to the top. Unlike Marlene, Mary reaches a moment of redemption at the play's end, seemingly brought about by her sudden, unexpected love for a child she never wanted, and once threatened to kill, but is persuaded to love by her much-exploited servant girl. In his review of the initial production, Michael Coveney cited the play's debt to Churchill: 'Following the example of Caryl Churchill and Howard Barker, Timberlake Wertenbaker sets her new play in the past [. . .] only to release her characters into the stormily consciousness-raised present' (*Financial Times*, 24 October 1985).

My Mother Said I Never Should (1987)

Published as: Keatley, Charlotte (2016), *My Mother Said I Never Should*. London: Methuen Drama.

There are several resonances between *Top Girls* and this play, which was first produced five years later, but written without Keatley's knowledge of her work's parallels to Churchill's. Most significant of these are the themes of difficult mother–daughter relationships, and the sometimes violent expression of these tensions. For example, just as Kit and Angie play in the backyard den, where Angie wishes in her opening line that her mother was dead and later threatens her murder, so the children who inhabit the 'wasteland' scenes of *My Mother Said I Never Should* fantasize about a plan to kill their mothers.

There is also a strong parallel between the ways in which Joyce has raised Angie as her own to allow Marlene to focus on her career in *Top Girls*, just as Margaret has raised Rosie, enabling Jackie to do the same in *My Mother Said I Never Should*. However, Jackie is a softer and more sympathetic character than Marlene: her struggles with this choice are more evident than Marlene's, and her actions do not leave any other character in the play so severely disadvantaged as Marlene's leave Angie and Joyce. In fact, it is Margaret who more clearly echoes Marlene's character when, in Act Three, Scene Two, she is surprised at her office by Rosie and Jackie returning from a holiday and struggles to accept the noise and colour they bring into her carefully ordered professional world, much as Marlene is taken aback by Angie's arrival at her agency.

The two plays also share some structural characteristics, such as a non-linear narrative and certain scenes which exist outside a naturalistic comprehension of time (such as the dinner party in *Top Girls* and the wasteland scenes in *My Mother Said I Never Should*).

Posh (2010)

Published as: Wade, Laura (2010), *Posh*. London: Oberon Books.

At first glance, this almost all-male play, which focusses on the exploits of a group of rich Oxbridge-educated young men at a university society dinner, might seem to bear little relation to Churchill's all-female examination of women's success and limitations. However, Wade's inverted image, which replaces Churchill's all-female dinner party with an equally drunken all-male one (both of which were first staged in the same theatrical setting at the Royal Court), clearly resonates with the earlier play. Interesting to compare are Churchill's and Wade's depictions of the disempowered waitress character: silent and ignored by women in *Top Girls*, and vocalized but molested by men in *Posh*.

Top Girls

Note on characters

ISABELLA BIRD (1831–1904) lived in Edinburgh, travelled extensively between the ages of forty and seventy.

LADY NIJO (b. 1258) Japanese, was an Emperor's courtesan and later a Buddhist nun who travelled on foot through Japan.

DULL GRET is the subject of the Brueghel painting, *Dulle Griet*, in which a woman in an apron and armour leads a crowd of women charging through hell and fighting the devils.

POPE JOAN, disguised as a man, is thought to have been Pope between 854–856.

PATIENT GRISELDA is the obedient wife whose story is told by Chaucer in 'The Clerk's Tale' of *The Canterbury Tales*.

Note on layout

A speech usually follows the one immediately before it BUT:

1: when one character starts speaking before the other has finished, the point of interruption is marked /.

e.g. **Isabella** This is the Emperor of Japan? / I once met the Emperor of Morocco.

    Nijo In fact he was the ex-Emperor.

2: a character sometimes continues speaking right through another's speech:

e.g. **Isabella** When I was forty I thought my life was over. / Oh I was pitiful. I was

    Nijo I didn't say I felt it for twenty years. Not every minute.

    Isabella sent on a cruise for my health and I felt even worse. Pains in my bones, pins and needles . . . etc.

3: sometimes a speech follows on from a speech earlier than the one immediately before it, and continuity is marked*.

e.g. **Griselda** I'd seen him riding by, we all had. And he'd seen me in the fields with the sheep*.

    Isabella I would have been well suited to minding sheep.

Nijo   And Mr Nugent riding by.

Isabella   Of course not, Nijo, I mean a healthy life in the open air.

Joan   *He just rode up while you were minding the sheep and asked you to marry him?

where 'in the fields with the sheep' is the cue to both 'I would have been' and 'He just rode up'.

Top Girls was first performed at the Royal Court Theatre, London, on 28 August 1982 with the following cast:

Marlene	Gwen Taylor
Isabella Bird **Joyce** **Mrs Kidd**	Deborah Findlay
Lady Nijo **Win**	Lindsay Duncan
Dull Gret **Angie**	Carole Hayman
Pope Joan **Louise**	Selina Cadell
Patient Griselda **Nell** **Jeanine**	Lesley Manville
Waitress **Kit** **Shona**	Lou Wakefield

Directed by Max Stafford Clark
Designed by Peter Hartwell

This production transferred to Joe Papp's Public Theatre, New York, later the same year, and returned to the Royal Court early in 1983.

ACT ONE	Restaurant. Saturday night.
ACT TWO	
Scene One:	Joyce's back yard. Sunday afternoon.
Scene Two:	'Top Girls' Employment agency. Monday morning.
ACT THREE	Joyce's kitchen. Sunday evening, a year earlier.

I originally wrote the play with this three-act structure – the dinner party, Angie goes to London, and a year earlier. For the first production at the Royal Court Theatre in 1982, it was decided that there should only be one interval and that the parts of Nell and Jeanine should be doubled, so the play was divided in the middle of Act II and one of the interviews was moved out of the main office scene. In earlier editions, I left the option of performing it as two or three acts, but left the interview scene in its new place. Since then, I have found I prefer the original simple structure, which has been used in several recent productions, and this is the way I would like the play to be performed in future. There is no need for two full-scale intervals, where the audience leave the theatre, if that is inconvenient – there can be a short break after Act I and a main interval after Act II, when we have had Saturday, Sunday and Monday and come to the chronological end of the play, before going back a year.

Caryl Churchill, May 2012

Act One

Restaurant. Table set for dinner with white tablecloth. Six places.
Marlene *and* **Waitress**.

Marlene   Excellent, yes, table for six. One of them's going to be
late but we won't wait. I'd like a bottle of Frascati straight away if
you've got one really cold.[1]

The **Waitress** *goes.*

Isabella Bird *arrives.*

Here we are. Isabella.

Isabella   Congratulations, my dear.

Marlene   Well, it's a step. It makes for a party. I haven't time for
a holiday. I'd like to go somewhere exotic like you but I can't get
away. I don't know how you could bear to leave Hawaii. / I'd like
to lie in the sun forever, except of course I

Isabella   I did think of settling.

Marlene   can't bear sitting still.

Isabella   I sent for my sister Hennie to come and join me. I said,
Hennie we'll live here forever and help the natives. You can buy
two sirloins of beef for what a pound of chops costs in Edinburgh.
And Hennie wrote back, the dear, that yes, she would come to
Hawaii if I wished, but I said she had far better stay where she was.
Hennie was suited to life in Tobermory.[2]

Marlene   Poor Hennie.

Isabella   Do you have a sister?

Marlene   Yes in fact.

Isabella   Hennie was happy. She was good. I did miss its face, my
own pet. But I couldn't stay in Scotland. I loathed the constant murk.

---

1   Frascati is a high-quality Italian white wine. Originating from the region around Rome, it
     was once favoured by popes.
2   A small coastal town on the Scottish island of Mull.

Marlene   Ah! Nijo!

She sees **Lady Nijo** *arrive.*

The **Waitress** *enters with wine.*

Nijo   Marlene!

Marlene   I think a drink while we wait for the others. I think a drink anyway. What a week.

The **Waitress** *pours wine.*

Nijo   It was always the men who used to get so drunk. I'd be one of the maidens, passing the sake.[3]

Isabella   I've had sake. Small hot drink. Quite fortifying after a day in the wet.

Nijo   One night my father proposed three rounds of three cups, which was normal, and then the Emperor should have said three rounds of three cups, but he said three rounds of nine cups, so you can imagine. Then the Emperor passed his sake cup to my father and said, 'Let the wild goose come to me this spring.'[4]

Marlene   Let the what?

Nijo   It's a literary allusion to a tenth-century epic, / His Majesty was very cultured.

Isabella   This is the Emperor of Japan? / I once met the Emperor of Morocco.

Nijo   In fact he was the ex-Emperor.

Marlene   But he wasn't old? / Did you, Isabella?

Nijo   Twenty-nine.

---

3   Sake is a potent Japanese rice wine.
4   A euphemistic metaphor meaning let Nijo (who might be considered a young, wild bird, yet to be tamed) come to his bed that spring. Although Nijo would still be considered a child by our standards, in her time and culture, the Emperor had the right to demand her from her father as his concubine (one of several women kept at court to provide the Emperor with sexual and other services, in addition to his wife). In fact, this request would have been seen as an honour.

Isabella   Oh it's a long story.

Marlene   Twenty-nine's an excellent age.

Nijo   Well I was only fourteen and I knew he meant something but I didn't know what. He sent me an eight-layered gown and I sent it back.[5] So when the time came I did nothing but cry. My thin gowns were badly ripped. But even that morning when he left / – he'd a green robe with a scarlet lining and

Marlene   Are you saying he raped you?

Nijo   very heavily embroidered trousers, I already felt different about him. It made me uneasy. No, of course not, Marlene, I belonged to him, it was what I was brought up for from a baby. I soon found I was sad if he stayed away. It was depressing day after day not knowing when he would come. I never enjoyed taking other women to him.

Isabella   I certainly never saw my father drunk. He was a clergyman. / And I didn't get married till I was fifty.

The **Waitress** *brings menus.*

Nijo   Oh, my father was a very religious man. Just before he died he said to me, 'Serve His Majesty, be respectful, if you lose his favour enter holy orders.'

Marlene   But he meant stay in a convent, not go wandering round the country.

Nijo   Priests were often vagrants, so why not a nun? You think I shouldn't? / I still did what my father wanted.

Marlene   No no, I think you should. / I think it was wonderful.

Dull Gret *arrives.*

Isabella   I tried to do what my father wanted.

---

5   In Japanese culture at this time, the wearing of multiple layered garments and certain materials and colour combinations denoted wealth and status, as is notable in Nijo's frequent references to clothes.

Marlene   Gret, good. Nijo. Gret. / I know Griselda's going to be late, but should we wait for Joan? / Let's get you a drink.

Isabella   Hello Gret! (*Continues to* **Nijo**.) I tried to be a clergyman's daughter. Needlework, music, charitable schemes. I had a tumour removed from my spine and spent a great deal of time on the sofa. I studied the metaphysical poets and hymnology.[6] / I thought I enjoyed intellectual pursuits.

Nijo   Ah, you like poetry. I come of a line of eight generations of poets. Father had a poem / in the anthology.

Isabella   My father taught me Latin although I was a girl.[7] / But

Marlene   They didn't have Latin at my school.

Isabella   really I was more suited to manual work. Cooking, washing, mending, riding horses. / Better than reading books,

Nijo   Oh but I'm sure you're very clever.

Isabella   eh Gret? A rough life in the open air.

Nijo   I can't say I enjoyed my rough life. What I enjoyed most was being the Emperor's favourite / and wearing thin silk.

Isabella   Did you have any horses, Gret?

Gret   Pig.

Pope Joan *arrives.*

Marlene   Oh Joan, thank God, we can order. Do you know everyone? We were just talking about learning Latin and being clever girls. Joan was by way of an infant prodigy. Of course you were. What excited you when you were ten?

---

6   Several seventeenth-century English poets, including John Donne, Andrew Marvell, George Herbert and Henry Vaughn, are regarded as metaphysical poets. Hymnology is the study of hymns.

7   In the nineteenth century, learning Latin was considered unfeminine and unnecessary for women.

Joan   Because angels are without matter they are not individuals. Every angel is a species.[8]

Marlene   There you are.

They laugh. They look at menus.

Isabella   Yes, I forgot all my Latin. But my father was the mainspring of my life and when he died I was so grieved. I'll have the chicken, please, / and the soup.[9]

Nijo   Of course you were grieved. My father was saying his prayers and he dozed off in the sun. So I touched his knee to rouse him. 'I wonder what will happen,' he said, and then he was dead before he finished the sentence. / If he'd died saying

Marlene   What a shock.

Nijo   his prayers he would have gone straight to heaven. / Waldorf salad.

Joan   Death is the return of all creatures to God.

Nijo   I shouldn't have woken him.

Joan   Damnation only means ignorance of the truth. I was always attracted by the teachings of John the Scot, though he was inclined to confuse / God and the world.[10]

Isabella   Grief always overwhelmed me at the time.

Marlene   What I fancy is a rare steak. Gret?

Isabella   I am of course a member of the / Church of England.*

Gret   Potatoes.

---

8   This refers to a theory proposed by St Thomas Aquinas in his *Summa Theologiae*. By 'without matter', Joan means without physical substance.

9   From this point onwards, the women's discussion is punctuated with their food orders, such as this one. Note that Churchill never gives a stage direction to instruct that the women speak directly to the Waitress. Rather, the implication is that they announce their orders regardless of her silent presence.

10 John the Scot was a ninth-century Irish theologian and philosopher who argued that the divine is intrinsically present throughout the natural universe.

Marlene   *I haven't been to church for years. / I like Christmas carols.

Isabella   Good works matter more than church attendance.

Marlene   Make that two steaks and a lot of potatoes. Rare. But I don't do good works either.

Joan   Canelloni, please, / and a salad.

Isabella   Well, I tried, but oh dear. Hennie did good works.

Nijo   The first half of my life was all sin and the second / all repentance.*

Marlene   Oh what about starters?

Gret   Soup.

Joan   *And which did you like best?

Marlene   Were your travels just a penance? Avocado vinaigrette. Didn't you / enjoy yourself?

Joan   Nothing to start with for me, thank you.

Nijo   Yes, but I was very unhappy. / It hurt to remember

Marlene   And the wine list.

Nijo   the past. I think that was repentance.

Marlene   Well I wonder.

Nijo   I might have just been homesick.

Marlene   Or angry.

Nijo   Not angry, no, / why angry?

Gret   Can we have some more bread?

Marlene   Don't you get angry? I get angry.

Nijo   But what about?

Marlene   Yes let's have two more Frascati. And some more bread, please.

The **Waitress** *exits.*

Isabella   I tried to understand Buddhism when I was in Japan but all this birth and death succeeding each other through eternities just filled me with the most profound melancholy.[11] I do like something more active.

Nijo   You couldn't say I was inactive. I walked every day for twenty years.

Isabella   I don't mean walking. / I mean in the head.

Nijo   I vowed to copy five Mahayana sutras.[12] / Do you know how

Marlene   I don't think religious beliefs are something we have in common. Activity yes.

Nijo   long they are? My head was active. / My head ached.

Joan   It's no good being active in heresy.

Isabella   What heresy? She's calling the Church of England / a heresy.

Joan   There are some very attractive / heresies.

Nijo   I had never heard of Christianity. Never / heard of it. Barbarians.

Marlene   Well I'm not a Christian. / And I'm not a Buddhist.

Isabella   You have heard of it?

Marlene   We don't all have to believe the same.

Isabella   I knew coming to dinner with a pope we should keep off religion.

Joan   I always enjoy a theological argument. But I won't try to convert you, I'm not a missionary. Anyway I'm a heresy myself.

Isabella   There are some barbaric practices in the east.

11   Isabella is referring to her limited Western understanding of the Buddhist belief in reincarnation.
12   Buddhist scriptures, which are thought by some to relate the teachings of the Buddha.

Nijo   Barbaric?

Isabella   Among the lower classes.

Nijo   I wouldn't know.

Isabella   Well theology always made my head ache.

Marlene   Oh good, some food.

Waitress *is bringing the first course.*

Nijo   How else could I have left the court if I wasn't a nun? When Father died I had only His Majesty. So when I fell out of favour I had nothing. Religion is a kind of nothing / and I dedicated what was left of me to nothing.

Isabella   That's what I mean about Buddhism. It doesn't brace.

Marlene   Come on, Nijo, have some wine.

Nijo   Haven't you ever felt like that? Nothing will ever happen again. I am dead already. You've all felt / like that.

Isabella   You thought your life was over but it wasn't.

Joan   You wish it was over.

Gret   Sad.

Marlene   Yes, when I first came to London I sometimes . . . and when I got back from America I did. But only for a few hours. Not twenty years.

Isabella   When I was forty I thought my life was over. / Oh I

Nijo   I didn't say I felt it for twenty years. Not every minute.

Isabella   was pitiful. I was sent on a cruise for my health and I felt even worse. Pains in my bones, pins and needles in my hands, swelling behind the ears, and – oh, stupidity. I shook all over, indefinable terror. And Australia seemed to me a hideous country, the acacias stank like drains. / I had a

Nijo   You were homesick.

Isabella   photograph for Hennie but I told her I wouldn't send it, my hair had fallen out and my clothes were crooked, I looked completely insane and suicidal.

Nijo   So did I, exactly, dressed as a nun. I was wearing walking shoes for the first time.

Isabella   I longed to go home, / but home to what? Houses

Nijo   I longed to go back ten years.

Isabella   are so perfectly dismal.

Marlene   I thought travelling cheered you both up.

Isabella   Oh it did / of course. It was on the trip from

Nijo   I'm not a cheerful person, Marlene. I just laugh a lot.

Isabella   Australia to the Sandwich Isles, I fell in love with the sea. There were rats in the cabin and ants in the food but suddenly it was like a new world. I woke up every morning happy, knowing there would be nothing to annoy me. No nervousness. No dressing.

Nijo   Don't you like getting dressed? I adored my clothes. / When I was chosen to give sake to His Majesty's brother,

Marlene   You had prettier colours than Isabella.

Nijo   the Emperor Kameyana, on his formal visit, I wore raw silk pleated trousers and a seven-layered gown in shades of red, and two outer garments, / yellow lined with green and a light

Marlene   Yes, all that silk must have been very . . .

The **Waitress** *starts to clear the first course.*

Joan   I dressed as a boy when I left home.*

Nijo   green jacket. Lady Betto had a five-layered gown in shades of green and purple.

Isabella   *You dressed as a boy?

Marlene   Of course, / for safety.

Joan   It was easy, I was only twelve. Also women weren't /
allowed in the library. We wanted to study in Athens.

Marlene   You ran away alone?

Joan   No, not alone, I went with my friend. / He was sixteen

Nijo   Ah, an elopement.

Joan   but I thought I knew more science than he did and almost
as much philosophy.

Isabella   Well I always travelled as a lady and I repudiated
strongly any suggestion in the press that I was other than feminine.

Marlene   I don't wear trousers in the office. / I could but I don't.

Isabella   There was no great danger to a woman of my age and
appearance.

Marlene   And you got away with it, Joan?

Joan   I did then.

The **Waitress** *starts to bring the main course.*

Marlene   And nobody noticed anything?

Joan   They noticed I was a very clever boy. / And when I

Marlene   I couldn't have kept pretending for so long.

Joan   shared a bed with my friend, that was ordinary – two poor
students in a lodging house. I think I forgot I was pretending.

Isabella   Rocky Mountain Jim, Mr Nugent, showed me no
disrespect.[13] He found it interesting, I think, that I could make
scones and also lasso cattle. Indeed he declared his love for me,
which was most distressing.

Nijo   What did he say? / We always sent poems first.

Marlene   What did you say?

13   Jim Nugent was a Colorado mountaineer, outlaw, army scout and poet.

Isabella   I urged him to give up whisky, / but he said it was too late.

Marlene   Oh Isabella.

Isabella   He had lived alone in the mountains for many years.

Marlene   But did you – ?

The **Waitress** *goes.*

Isabella   Mr Nugent was a man that any woman might love but none could marry. I came back to England.

Nijo   Did you write him a poem when you left? / Snow on the

Marlene   Did you never see him again?

Isabella   No, never.

Nijo   mountains. My sleeves are wet with tears. In England no tears, no snow.

Isabella   Well, I say never. One morning very early in Switzerland, it was a year later, I had a vision of him as I last saw him / in his trapper's clothes with his hair round his face,

Nijo   A ghost!

Isabella   and that was the day, / I learnt later, he died with a

Nijo   Ah!

Isabella   bullet in his brain. / He just bowed to me and vanished.

Marlene   Oh Isabella.

Nijo   When your lover dies – One of my lovers died. / The priest Ariake.

Joan   My friend died. Have we all got dead lovers?

Marlene   Not me, sorry.

Nijo (*to* **Isabella**)   I wasn't a nun, I was still at court, but he was a priest, and when he came to me he dedicated his whole life to hell. / He knew that when he died he would fall into one of the three lower realms. And he died, he did die.

Joan (*to* **Marlene**)   I'd quarrelled with him over the teachings of John the Scot, who held that our ignorance of God is the same as his ignorance of himself. He only knows what he creates because he creates everything he knows but he himself is above being – do you follow?

Marlene   No, but go on.

Nijo   I couldn't bear to think / in what shape would he be reborn.*

Joan   St Augustine maintained that the Neo-Platonic Ideas are indivisible from God, but I agreed with John that the created

Isabella   *Buddhism is really most uncomfortable.

Joan   world is essences derived from Ideas which derived from God. As Denys the Areopagite said – the pseudo-Denys – first we give God a name, then deny it / then reconcile the

Nijo   In what shape would he return?

Joan   contradiction by looking beyond / those terms.[14]

Marlene   Sorry, what? Denys said what?

Joan   Well we disagreed about it, we quarrelled. And next day he was ill, / I was so annoyed with him, all the time I was

Nijo   Misery in this life and worse in the next, all because of me.

Joan   nursing him I kept going over the arguments in my mind. Matter is not a means of knowing the essence. The source of the species is the Idea. But then I realised he'd never understand my arguments again, and that night he died. John the Scot held that the individual disintegrates / and there is no personal immortality.

Isabella   I wouldn't have you think I was in love with Jim Nugent. It was yearning to save him that I felt.

Marlene (*to* **Joan**)   So what did you do?

---

14   St Augustine (also known as Augustine of Hippo) and Denys the Areopagite were early (fifth-century) Christian theologians and philosophers. Neo-Platonic philosophy holds that everything in existence derives from a single source, and was thus incorporated into much Christian thinking.

Joan   First I decided to stay a man. I was used to it. And I wanted to devote my life to learning. Do you know why I went to Rome? Italian men didn't have beards.

Isabella   The loves of my life were Hennie, my own pet, and my dear husband the doctor, who nursed Hennie in her last illness. I knew it would be terrible when Hennie died but I didn't know how terrible. I felt half of myself had gone. How could I go on my travels without that sweet soul waiting at home for my letters? It was Doctor Bishop's devotion to her in her last illness that made me decide to marry him. He and Hennie had the same sweet character. I had not.

Nijo   I thought His Majesty had a sweet character because when he found out about Ariake he was so kind. But really it was because he no longer cared for me. One night he even sent me out to a man who had been pursuing me. / He lay awake on the other side of the screens and listened.

Isabella   I did wish marriage had seemed more of a step. I tried very hard to cope with the ordinary drudgery of life. I was ill again with carbuncles on the spine and nervous prostration. I ordered a tricycle, that was my idea of adventure then. And John himself fell ill, with erysipelas and anaemia.[15] I began to love him with my whole heart but it was too late. He was a skeleton with transparent white hands. I wheeled him on various seafronts in a bathchair. And he faded and left me. There was nothing in my life. The doctors said I had gout / and my heart was much affected.

Nijo   There was nothing in my life, nothing, without the Emperor's favour. The Empress had always been my enemy, Marlene, she said I had no right to wear three-layered gowns. / But I was the adopted daughter of my grandfather the Prime Minister. I had been publicly granted permission to wear thin silk.

---

15 Carbuncles are clusters of painful boils, which can cause the sufferer to feel weak and exhausted; nervous prostration is another term for nervous exhaustion or a nervous breakdown; erysipelas is an acute skin infection; anaemia is a blood condition, usually caused by iron deficiency, which causes tiredness and weakness; gout is a painful inflammation of the joints.

Joan   There was nothing in my life except my studies. I was obsessed with pursuit of the truth. I taught at the Greek School in Rome, which St Augustine had made famous. I was poor, I worked hard. I spoke apparently brilliantly, I was still very young, I was a stranger; suddenly I was quite famous, I was everyone's favourite. Huge crowds came to hear me. The day after they made me cardinal I fell ill and lay two weeks without speaking, full of terror and regret. / But then I got up

Marlene   Yes, success is very . . .

Joan   determined to go on. I was seized again / with a desperate longing for the absolute.

Isabella   Yes, yes, to go on. I sat in Tobermory among Hennie's flowers and sewed a complete outfit in Jaeger flannel.[16] / I was fifty-six years old.

Nijo   Out of favour but I didn't die. I left on foot, nobody saw me go. For the next twenty years I walked through Japan.

Gret   Walking is good.

The **Waitress** *enters.*

Joan   Pope Leo died and I was chosen. All right then. I would be Pope. I would know God. I would know everything.

Isabella   I determined to leave my grief behind and set off for Tibet.

Marlene   Magnificent all of you. We need some more wine, please, two bottles I think, Griselda isn't even here yet, and I want to drink a toast to you all.

Isabella   To yourself surely, / we're here to celebrate your success.

Nijo   Yes, Marlene.

Joan   Yes, what is it exactly, Marlene?

16   A brand of woollen clothing and cloth, founded with a belief in the health-giving effects of wearing animal fibres close to the skin.

Marlene   Well it's not Pope but it is managing director.*

Joan   And you find work for people.

Marlene   Yes, an employment agency.

Nijo   *Over all the women you work with. And the men.

Isabella   And very well deserved too. I'm sure it's just the beginning of something extraordinary.

Marlene   Well it's worth a party.

Isabella   To Marlene.*

Marlene   And all of us.

Joan   *Marlene.

Nijo   Marlene.

Gret   Marlene.

Marlene   We've all come a long way. To our courage and the way we changed our lives and our extraordinary achievements.

They laugh and drink a toast.

Isabella   Such adventures. We were crossing a mountain pass at seven thousand feet, the cook was all to pieces, the muleteers suffered fever and snow blindness.[17] But even though my spine was agony I managed very well.

Marlene   Wonderful.

Nijo   Once I was ill for four months lying alone at an inn. Nobody to offer a horse to Buddha. I had to live for myself, and I did live.

Isabella   Of course you did. It was far worse returning to Tobermory. I always felt dull when I was stationary. / That's why I could never stay anywhere.

---

17   A muleteer is someone who drives (keeps and leads) mules (the offspring of a horse and a donkey often used to carry goods and possessions on journeys).

Nijo   Yes, that's it exactly. New sights. The shrine by the beach, the moon shining on the sea. The goddess had vowed to save all living things. / She would even save the fishes. I was full of hope.

Joan   I had thought the Pope would know everything. I thought God would speak to me directly. But of course he knew I was a woman.

Marlene   But nobody else even suspected?

The **Waitress** *brings more wine.*

Joan   In the end I did take a lover again.*

Isabella   In the Vatican?

Gret   *Keep you warm.

Nijo   *Ah, lover.

Marlene   *Good for you.

Joan   He was one of my chamberlains. There are such a lot of servants when you're a Pope. The food's very good. And I realised I did know the truth. Because whatever the Pope says, that's true.

Nijo   What was he like, the chamberlain?*

Gret   Big cock.

Isabella   Oh Gret.

Marlene   *Did he fancy you when he thought you were a fella?

Nijo   What was he like?

Joan   He could keep a secret.

Marlene   So you did know everything.

Joan   Yes, I enjoyed being Pope. I consecrated bishops and let people kiss my feet. I received the King of England when he came to submit to the church. Unfortunately there were earthquakes, and some village reported it had rained blood, and in France there was a plague of giant grasshoppers, but I don't think that can have been my fault, do you?*

Laughter.

The grasshoppers fell on the English Channel and were washed up on shore and their bodies rotted and poisoned the air and everyone in those parts died.

Laughter.

Isabella   *Such superstition! I was nearly murdered in China by a howling mob. They thought the barbarians ate babies and put them under railway sleepers to make the tracks steady, and ground up their eyes to make the lenses of cameras. / So

Marlene   And you had a camera!

Isabella   they were shouting, 'child-eater, child-eater'. Some people tried to sell girl babies to Europeans for cameras or stew!

Laughter.

Marlene   So apart from the grasshoppers it was a great success.

Joan   Yes, if it hadn't been for the baby I expect I'd have lived to an old age like Theodora of Alexandria, who lived as a monk. She was accused by a girl / who fell in love with her of being the father of her child and –

Nijo   But tell us what happened to your baby. I had some babies.

Marlene   Didn't you think of getting rid of it?

Joan   Wouldn't that be a worse sin than having it? / But a Pope with a child was about as bad as possible.

Marlene   I don't know, you're the Pope.

Joan   But I wouldn't have known how to get rid of it.

Marlene   Other Popes had children, surely.

Joan   They didn't give birth to them.

Nijo   Well you were a woman.

Joan   Exactly and I shouldn't have been a woman. Women, children and lunatics can't be Pope.

Marlene   So the only thing to do / was to get rid of it somehow.

Nijo   You had to have it adopted secretly.

Joan   But I didn't know what was happening. I thought I was getting fatter, but then I was eating more and sitting about, the life of a Pope is quite luxurious. I don't think I'd spoken to a woman since I was twelve. The chamberlain was the one who realised.

Marlene   And by then it was too late.

Joan   Oh I didn't want to pay attention. It was easier to do nothing.

Nijo   But you had to plan for having it. You had to say you were ill and go away.

Joan   That's what I should have done I suppose.

Marlene   Did you want them to find out?

Nijo   I too was often in embarrassing situations, there's no need for a scandal. My first child was His Majesty's, which unfortunately died, but my second was Akebono's. I was seventeen. He was in love with me when I was thirteen, he was very upset when I had to go to the Emperor, it was very romantic, a lot of poems. Now His Majesty hadn't been near me for two months so he thought I was four months pregnant when I was really six, so when I reached the ninth month / I

Joan   I never knew what month it was.

Nijo   announced I was seriously ill, and Akebono announced he had gone on a religious retreat. He held me round the waist and lifted me up as the baby was born. He cut the cord with a short sword, wrapped the baby in white and took it away. It was only a girl but I was sorry to lose it. Then I told the Emperor that the baby had miscarried because of my illness, and there you are. The danger was past.

Joan   But Nijo, I wasn't used to having a woman's body.

Isabella   So what happened?

Joan   I didn't know of course that it was near the time. It was Rogation Day, there was always a procession.[18] I was on the horse dressed in my robes and a cross was carried in front of me, and all the cardinals were following, and all the clergy of Rome, and a huge crowd of people. / We set off from

Marlene   Total Pope.

Joan   St Peter's to go to St John's. I had felt a slight pain earlier, I thought it was something I'd eaten, and then it came back, and came back more often. I thought when this is over I'll go to bed. There were still long gaps when I felt perfectly all right and I didn't want to attract attention to myself and spoil the ceremony. Then I suddenly realised what it must be. I had to last out till I could get home and hide. Then something changed, my breath started to catch, I couldn't plan things properly any more. We were in a little street that goes between St Clement's and the Colosseum, and I just had to get off the horse and sit down for a minute. Great waves of pressure were going through my body, I heard sounds like a cow lowing, they came out of my mouth. Far away I heard people screaming, 'The Pope is ill, the Pope is dying.' And the baby just slid out onto the road.*

Marlene   The cardinals / won't have known where to put themselves.

Nijo   Oh dear, Joan, what a thing to do! In the street!

Isabella   *How embarrassing.

Gret   In a field, yah.

They are laughing.

Joan   One of the cardinals said, 'The Antichrist!' and fell over in a faint.

They all laugh.

Marlene   So what did they do? They weren't best pleased.

18   In the Catholic Church, Rogation Days are days of prayer, fasting and procession to ask for God's protection.

Joan   They took me by the feet and dragged me out of town and stoned me to death.

They stop laughing.

Marlene   Joan, how horrible.

Joan   I don't really remember.

Nijo   And the child died too?

Joan   Oh yes, I think so, yes.

Pause.

*The **Waitress** enters to clear the plates. They start talking quietly.*

Isabella (*to* **Joan**)   I never had any children. I was very fond of horses.

Nijo (*to* **Marlene**)   I saw my daughter once. She was three years old. She wore a plum-red / small-sleeved gown. Akebono's

Isabella   Birdie was my favourite. A little Indian bay mare I rode in the Rocky Mountains.

Nijo   wife had taken the child because her own died. Everyone thought I was just a visitor. She was being brought up carefully so she could be sent to the palace like I was.

Isabella   Legs of iron and always cheerful, and such a pretty face. If a stranger led her she reared up like a bronco.[19]

Nijo   I never saw my third child after he was born, the son of Ariake the priest. Ariake held him on his lap the day he was born and talked to him as if he could understand, and cried. My fourth child was Ariake's too. Ariake died before he was born. I didn't want to see anyone, I stayed alone in the hills. It was a boy again, my third son. But oddly enough I felt nothing for him.

Marlene   How many children did you have, Gret?

Gret   Ten.

19 An untrained horse.

Isabella   Whenever I came back to England I felt I had so much to atone for. Hennie and John were so good. I did no good in my life. I spent years in self-gratification. So I hurled myself into committees, I nursed the people of Tobermory in the epidemic of influenza, I lectured the Young Women's Christian Association on Thrift. I talked and talked explaining how the East was corrupt and vicious. My travels must do good to someone beside myself. I wore myself out with good causes.

Marlene   Oh God, why are we all so miserable?

Joan   The procession never went down that street again.

Marlene   They rerouted it specially?

Joan   Yes they had to go all round to avoid it. And they introduced a pierced chair.

Marlene   A pierced chair?

Joan   Yes, a chair made out of solid marble with a hole in the seat / and it was in the Chapel of the Saviour, and after he was

Marlene   You're not serious.

Joan   elected the Pope had to sit in it.

Marlene   And someone looked up his skirts? Not really?

Isabella   What an extraordinary thing.

Joan   Two of the clergy / made sure he was a man.

Nijo   On their hands and knees!

Marlene   A pierced chair!

Gret   Balls!

Griselda *arrives unnoticed.*

Nijo   Why couldn't he just pull up his robe?

Joan   He had to sit there and look dignified.

Marlene   You could have made all your chamberlains sit in it.*

Gret   Big one, small one.

Nijo   Very useful chair at court.

Isabella   *Or the laird of Tobermory in his kilt.

They are quite drunk. They get the giggles.

Marlene *notices* **Griselda**.

Marlene   Griselda! / There you are. Do you want to eat?

Griselda   I'm sorry I'm so late. No, no, don't bother.

Marlene   Of course it's no bother. / Have you eaten?

Griselda   No really, I'm not hungry.

Marlene   Well have some pudding.

Griselda   I never eat pudding.

Marlene   Griselda, I hope you're not anorexic. We're having pudding, I am, and getting nice and fat.

Griselda   Oh if everyone is. I don't mind.

Marlene   Now who do you know? This is Joan who was Pope in the ninth century, and Isabella Bird, the Victorian traveller, and Lady Nijo from Japan, Emperor's concubine and Buddhist nun, thirteenth century, nearer your own time, and Gret who was painted by Brueghel. Griselda's in Boccaccio and Petrarch and Chaucer because of her extraordinary marriage.[20] I'd like profiteroles because they're disgusting.

Joan   Zabaglione, please.

Isabella   Apple pie / and cream.

Nijo   What's this?

---

20 Brueghel was a sixteenth-century Dutch artist. Dull Gret features in his 1562 painting 'Dulle Griet', which mocks the idea of women obtaining power or a voice in society. Boccaccio and Petrarch were fourteenth-century Italian writers. Griselda features in Boccaccio's *The Decameron*, which Petrarch translated into Latin. Not long after, her story also featured as *The Clerk's Tale* in the English poet Chaucer's *The Canterbury Tales*.

Marlene   Zabaglione, it's Italian, it's what Joan's having, / it's delicious.

Nijo   A Roman Catholic / dessert? Yes please.

Marlene   Gret?

Gret   Cake.

Griselda   Just cheese and biscuits, thank you.

Marlene   Yes, Griselda's life is like a fairy-story, except it starts with marrying the prince.

Griselda   He's only a marquis, Marlene.

Marlene   Well everyone for miles around is his liege and he's absolute lord of life and death and you were the poor but beautiful peasant girl and he whisked you off. / Near enough a prince.

Nijo   How old were you?

Griselda   Fifteen.

Nijo   I was brought up in court circles and it was still a shock. Had you ever seen him before?

Griselda   I'd seen him riding by, we all had. And he'd seen me in the fields with the sheep.*

Isabella   I would have been well suited to minding sheep.

Nijo   And Mr Nugent riding by.

Isabella   Of course not, Nijo, I mean a healthy life in the open air.

Joan   *He just rode up while you were minding the sheep and asked you to marry him?

Griselda   No, no, it was on the wedding day. I was waiting outside the door to see the procession. Everyone wanted him to get married so there'd be an heir to look after us when he died, / and at last he announced a day for the wedding but

Marlene   I don't think Walter wanted to get married. It is Walter? Yes.

Griselda   nobody knew who the bride was, we thought it must be a foreign princess, we were longing to see her. Then the carriage stopped outside our cottage and we couldn't see the bride anywhere. And he came and spoke to my father.

Nijo   And your father told you to serve the Prince.

Griselda   My father could hardly speak. The Marquis said it wasn't an order, I could say no, but if I said yes I must always obey him in everything.

Marlene   That's when you should have suspected.

Griselda   But of course a wife must obey her husband. / And of course I must obey the Marquis.*

Isabella   I swore to obey dear John, of course, but it didn't seem to arise. Naturally I wouldn't have wanted to go abroad while I was married.

Marlene   *Then why bother to mention it at all? He'd got a thing about it, that's why.

Griselda   I'd rather obey the Marquis than a boy from the village.

Marlene   Yes, that's a point.

Joan   I never obeyed anyone. They all obeyed me.

Nijo   And what did you wear? He didn't make you get married in your own clothes? That would be perverse.*

Marlene   Oh, you wait.

Griselda   *He had ladies with him who undressed me and they had a white silk dress and jewels for my hair.

Marlene   And at first he seemed perfectly normal?

Griselda   Marlene, you're always so critical of him. / Of course he was normal, he was very kind.

Marlene   But Griselda, come on, he took your baby.

Griselda   Walter found it hard to believe I loved him. He couldn't believe I would always obey him. He had to prove it.

Marlene   I don't think Walter likes women.

Griselda   I'm sure he loved me, Marlene, all the time.

Marlene   He just had a funny way / of showing it.

Griselda   It was hard for him too.

Joan   How do you mean he took away your baby?

Nijo   Was it a boy?

Griselda   No, the first one was a girl.

Nijo   Even so it's hard when they take it away. Did you see it at all?

Griselda   Oh yes, she was six weeks old.

Nijo   Much better to do it straight away.

Isabella   But why did your husband take the child?

Griselda   He said all the people hated me because I was just one of them. And now I had a child they were restless. So he had to get rid of the child to keep them quiet. But he said he wouldn't snatch her, I had to agree and obey and give her up. So when I was feeding her a man came in and took her away. I thought he was going to kill her even before he was out of the room.

Marlene   But you let him take her? You didn't struggle?

Griselda   I asked him to give her back so I could kiss her. And I asked him to bury her where no animals could dig her up. / It

Isabella   Oh my dear.

Griselda   was Walter's child to do what he liked with.*

Marlene   Walter was bonkers.

Gret   Bastard.

Isabella   *But surely, murder.

Griselda   I had promised.

Marlene   I can't stand this. I'm going for a pee.

Marlene *goes out.*

The **Waitress** *brings dessert.*

Nijo   No, I understand. Of course you had to, he was your life. And were you in favour after that?

Griselda   Oh yes, we were very happy together. We never spoke about what had happened.

Isabella   I can see you were doing what you thought was your duty. But didn't it make you ill?

Griselda   No, I was very well, thank you.

Nijo   And you had another child?

Griselda   Not for four years, but then I did, yes, a boy.

Nijo   Ah a boy. / So it all ended happily.

Griselda   Yes he was pleased. I kept my son till he was two years old. A peasant's grandson. It made the people angry. Walter explained.

Isabella   But surely he wouldn't kill his children / just because –

Griselda   Oh it wasn't true. Walter would never give in to the people. He wanted to see if I loved him enough.

Joan   He killed his children / to see if you loved him enough?

Nijo   Was it easier the second time or harder?

Griselda   It was always easy because I always knew I would do what he said.

Pause. They start to eat.

Isabella   I hope you didn't have any more children.

Griselda   Oh no, no more. It was twelve years till he tested me again.

Isabella   So whatever did he do this time? / My poor John, I never loved him enough, and he would never have dreamt . . .

Griselda   He sent me away. He said the people wanted him to marry someone else who'd give him an heir and he'd got special permission from the Pope. So I said I'd go home to my father. I came with nothing / so I went with nothing. I

Nijo   Better to leave if your master doesn't want you.

Griselda   took off my clothes. He let me keep a slip so he wouldn't be shamed. And I walked home barefoot. My father came out in tears. Everyone was crying except me.

Nijo   At least your father wasn't dead. / I had nobody.

Isabella   Well it can be a relief to come home. I loved to see Hennie's sweet face again.

Griselda   Oh yes, I was perfectly content. And quite soon he sent for me again.

Joan   I don't think I would have gone.

Griselda   But he told me to come. I had to obey him. He wanted me to help prepare his wedding. He was getting married to a young girl from France / and nobody except me knew how to arrange things the way he liked them.

Nijo   It's always hard taking him another woman.

Marlene *comes back.*

Joan   I didn't live a woman's life. I don't understand it.

Griselda   The girl was sixteen and far more beautiful than me. I could see why he loved her. / She had her younger brother with her as a page.

The **Waitress** *enters.*

Marlene   Oh God, I can't bear it. I want some coffee. Six coffees. Six brandies. / Double brandies. Straight away.

Griselda   They all went in to the feast I'd prepared. And he stayed behind, and put his arms round me and kissed me. / I felt half asleep with the shock.

Nijo   Oh, like a dream.

Marlene   And he said, 'This is your daughter and your son.'

Griselda   Yes.

Joan   What?

Nijo   Oh. Oh I see. You got them back.

Isabella   I did think it was remarkably barbaric to kill them but you learn not to say anything. / So he had them brought up secretly I suppose.

Marlene   Walter's a monster. Weren't you angry? What did you do?

Griselda   Well I fainted. Then I cried and kissed the children. / Everyone was making a fuss of me.

Nijo   But did you feel anything for them?

Griselda   What?

Nijo   Did you feel anything for the children?

Griselda   Of course, I loved them.

Joan   So you forgave him and lived with him?

Griselda   He suffered so much all those years.

Isabella   Hennie had the same sweet nature.

Nijo   So they dressed you again?

Griselda   Cloth of gold.

Joan   I can't forgive anything.

Marlene   You really are exceptional, Griselda.

Nijo   Nobody gave me back my children.

Nijo *cries. The* **Waitress** *brings brandies.*

Isabella   I can never be like Hennie. I was always so busy in England, a kind of business I detested. The very presence of people exhausted my emotional reserves. I could not be like Hennie however I tried. I tried and was as ill as could be. The doctor suggested a steel net to support my head, the weight of my own head was too much for my diseased spine. / It is dangerous to put oneself in depressing circumstances. Why should I do it?

Joan   Don't cry.

Nijo   My father and the Emperor both died in the autumn. So much pain.

Joan   Yes, but don't cry.

Nijo   They wouldn't let me into the palace when he was dying. I hid in the room with his coffin, then I couldn't find where I'd left my shoes, I ran after the funeral procession in bare feet, I couldn't keep up. When I got there it was over, a few wisps of smoke in the sky, that's all that was left of him. What I want to know is, if I'd still been at court, would I have been allowed to wear full mourning?

Marlene   I'm sure you would.

Nijo   Why do you say that? You don't know anything about it. Would I have been allowed to wear full mourning?

Isabella   How can people live in this dim pale island and wear our hideous clothes? I cannot and will not live the life of a lady.

Nijo   I'll tell you something that made me angry. I was eighteen, at the Full Moon Ceremony. They make a special rice gruel and stir it with their sticks, and then they beat their women across the loins so they'll have sons and not daughters. So the Emperor beat us all / very hard as usual – that's not it,

Marlene   What a sod.

Nijo   Marlene, that's normal, what made us angry, he told his attendants they could beat us too. Well they had a wonderful time. / So Lady Genki and I made a plan, and the ladies all hid

The **Waitress** *has entered with coffees.*

Marlene   I'd like another brandy please. Better make it six.

Nijo   in his rooms, and Lady Mashimizu stood guard with a stick at the door, and when His Majesty came in Genki seized him and I beat him till he cried out and promised he would never order anyone to hit us again. Afterwards there was a terrible fuss. The nobles were horrified. 'We wouldn't even dream of stepping on your Majesty's shadow.' And I had hit him with a stick. Yes, I hit him with a stick.

Joan   Suave, mari magno turbantibus aequora ventis,
e terra magnum alterius spectare laborem;
non quia vexari quemquamst iucunda voluptas,
sed quibus ipse malis careas quia cernere suave est.
Suave etiam belli certamina magna tueri
per campos instructa tua sine parte pericli.
Sed nil dulcius est, bene quam munita tenere
edita doctrina sapientum templa serena, /
despicere unde queas alios passimque videre
errare atquc viam palantis quaerere vitae,

Griselda   I do think – I do wonder – it would have been nicer if Walter hadn't had to.

Isabella   Why should I? Why should I?

Marlene   Of course not.

Nijo   I hit him with a stick.

Joan   certare ingenio, contendere nobilitate,
noctes atque dies niti praestante labore
ad summas emergere opes retumque potiri.
O miseras / hominum mentis, I pectora caeca!*

Isabella   Oh miseras!

Nijo   *Pectora caeca.

Joan   qualibus in tenebris vitae quantisque periclis
degitur hoc aevi quodcumquest! / nonne videre
nil aliud sibi naturam latrare, nisi utqui
corpore seiunctus dolor absit, mente fruatur.[21]

---

21   Joan is reciting at length, in Latin, from the Roman poet and philosopher Lucretius' *De rerum natura* (*On the Nature of Things*), which argues against the fear of God and death, and for the explanation of the world through natural laws. However, this passage reflects on the pleasure of withdrawing from worldly pain and struggles.

Joan *subsides*.

Gret   We come into hell through a big mouth. Hell's black and red. / It's like the village where I come from. There's a river and

Marlene (*to* **Joan**)   Shut up, pet.

Isabella   Listen, she's been to hell.

Gret   a bridge and houses. There's places on fire like when the soldiers come. There's a big devil sat on a roof with a big hole in his arse and he's scooping stuff out of it with a big ladle and it's falling down on us, and it's money, so a lot of the women stop and get some. But most of us is fighting the devils. There's lots of little devils, our size, and we get them down all right and give them a beating. There's lots of funny creatures round your feet, you don't like to look, like rats and lizards, and nasty things, a bum with a face, and fish with legs, and faces on things that don't have faces on. But they don't hurt, you just keep going. Well we'd had worse, you see, we'd had the Spanish. We'd all had family killed. My big son die on a wheel.[22] Birds eat him. My baby, a soldier run her through with a sword. I'd had enough, I was mad, I hate the bastards. I come out my front door that morning and shout till my neighbours come out and I said, 'Come on, we're going where the evil come from and pay the bastards out.' And they all come out just as they was / from baking or washing in their

Nijo   All the ladies come.

Gret   aprons, and we push down the street and the ground opens up and we go through a big mouth into a street just like ours but in hell. I've got a sword in my hand from somewhere and I fill a basket with gold cups they drink out of down there. You just keep running on and fighting / you didn't stop for nothing. Oh we give them devils such a beating.

---

22   For long swathes of the sixteenth and seventeenth centuries, large sections of the Netherlands were at war with/in rebellion against the Spanish regime that ruled them. For ordinary people like Gret and her family, this was a dangerous and violent time. It appears that her son has been executed by being strapped to a cart wheel and beaten to death, a relatively common method of execution at this time.

Nijo   Take that, take that.

Joan   Something something something mortisque timores tum vacuum pectus – damn.

Quod si ridicula –

something something on and on and on and something splendorem pupureai.

Isabella   I thought I would have a last jaunt up the west river in China. Why not? But the doctors were so very grave. I just went to Morocco. The sea was so wild I had to be landed by ship's crane in a coal bucket. / My horse was a terror to me a

Gret   Coal bucket, good.

Joan   nos in luce timemus

something

terrorem.

Isabella   powerful black charger.

Nijo *is laughing and crying.*

Joan *gets up and is sick in a corner.*

Marlene *is drinking* **Isabella***'s brandy.*

So off I went to visit the Berber sheikhs in full blue trousers and great brass spurs.[23] I was the only European woman ever to have seen the Emperor of Morocco. I was seventy years old. What lengths to go to for a last chance of joy. I knew my return of vigour was only temporary, but how marvellous while it lasted.

---

23 Berbers are an ethnic group from northern Africa. Their leaders are called Sheiks.

Act Two

Scene One

Joyce's *back yard. The house with back door is upstage. Downstage a shelter made of junk, made by children. Two girls,* **Angie** *and* **Kit***, are in it, squashed together.* **Angie** *is sixteen,* **Kit** *is twelve. They cannot be seen from the house.* **Joyce** *calls from the house.*

Joyce   Angie. Angie are you out there?

Silence. They keep still and wait. When nothing else happens they relax.

Angie   Wish she was dead.

Kit   Wanna watch *The Exterminator*?[24]

Angie   You're sitting on my leg.

Kit   There's nothing on telly. We can have an ice cream. Angie?

Angie   Shall I tell you something?

Kit   Do you wanna watch *The Exterminator*?

Angie   It's X, innit.[25]

Kit   I can get into Xs.

Angie   Shall I tell you something?

Kit   We'll go to something else. We'll go to Ipswich. What's on the Odeon?

Angie   She won't let me, will she?

Kit   Don't tell her.

Angie   I've no money.

Kit   I'll pay.

24   A violent American action film of 1980.
25   At this time, films rated suitable for eighteen years and over were given an 'X' rating.

Angie   She'll moan though, won't she?

Kit   I'll ask her for you if you like.

Angie   I've no money, I don't want you to pay.

Kit   I'll ask her.

Angie   She don't like you.

Kit   I still got three pounds birthday money. Did she say she don't like me? I'll go by myself then.

Angie   Your mum don't let you. I got to take you.

Kit   She won't know.

Angie   You'd be scared who'd sit next to you.

Kit   No I wouldn't.
She does like me anyway.
Tell me then.

Angie   Tell you what?

Kit   It's you she doesn't like.

Angie   Well I don't like her so tough shit.

Joyce (*off*)   Angie. Angie. Angie. I know you're out there. I'm not coming out after you. You come in here.

Silence. Nothing happens.

Angie   Last night when I was in bed. I been thinking yesterday could I make things move. You know, make things move by thinking about them without touching them. Last night I was in bed and suddenly a picture fell down off the wall.

Kit   What picture?

Angie   My gran, that picture. Not the poster. The photograph in the frame.

Kit   Had you done something to make it fall down?

Angie   I must have done.

Kit   But were you thinking about it?

Angie   Not about it, but about something.

Kit   I don't think that's very good.

Angie   You know the kitten?

Kit   Which one?

Angie   There only is one. The dead one.

Kit   What about it?

Angie   I heard it last night.

Kit   Where?

Angie   Out here. In the dark. What if I left you here in the dark all night?

Kit   You couldn't. I'd go home.

Angie   You couldn't.

Kit   I'd / go home.

Angie   No you couldn't, not if I said.

Kit   I could.

Angie   Then you wouldn't see anything. You'd just be ignorant.

Kit   I can see in the daytime.

Angie   No you can't. You can't hear it in the daytime.

Kit   I don't want to hear it.

Angie   You're scared that's all.

Kit   I'm not scared of anything.

Angie   You're scared of blood.

Kit   It's not the same kitten anyway. You just heard an old cat, / you just heard some old cat.

Angie   You don't know what I heard. Or what I saw. You don't know nothing because you're a baby.

Kit   You're sitting on me.

Angie   Mind my hair / you silly cunt.

Kit   Stupid fucking cow, I hate you.

Angie   I don't care if you do.

Kit   You're horrible.

Angie   I'm going to kill my mother and you're going to watch.

Kit   I'm not playing.

Angie   You're scared of blood.

Kit *puts her hand under her dress, brings it out with blood on her finger.*

Kit   There, see, I got my own blood, so.

Angie *takes* **Kit***'s hand and licks her finger.*

Angie   Now I'm a cannibal. I might turn into a vampire now.

Kit   That picture wasn't nailed up right.

Angie   You'll have to do that when I get mine.

Kit   I don't have to.

Angie   You're scared.

Kit   I'll do it, I might do it. I don't have to just because you say. I'll be sick on you.

Angie   I don't care if you are sick on me, I don't mind sick. I don't mind blood. If I don't get away from here I'm going to die.

Kit   I'm going home.

Angie   You can't go through the house. She'll see you.

Kit   I won't tell her.

Angie   Oh great, fine.

Kit   I'll say I was by myself. I'll tell her you're at my house and I'm going there to get you.

Angie   She knows I'm here, stupid.

Kit   Then why can't I go through the house?

Angie   Because I said not.

Kit   My mum don't like you anyway.

Angie   I don't want her to like me. She's a slag.

Kit   She is not.

Angie   She does it with everyone.

Kit   She does not.

Angie   You don't even know what it is.

Kit   Yes I do.

Angie   Tell me then.

Kit   We get it all at school, cleverclogs. It's on television. You haven't done it.

Angie   How do you know?

Kit   Because I know you haven't.

Angie   You know wrong then because I have.

Kit   Who with?

Angie   I'm not telling you / who with.

Kit   You haven't anyway.

Angie   How do you know?

Kit   Who with?

Angie   I'm not telling you.

Kit   You said you told me everything.

Angie   I was lying wasn't I?

Kit   Who with? You can't tell me who with because / you never –

Angie   Sh.

Joyce *has come out of the house. She stops halfway across the yard and listens. They listen.*

Joyce   You there Angie? Kit? You there Kitty? Want a cup of tea? I've got some chocolate biscuits. Come on now I'll put the kettle on. Want a choccy biccy, Angie?

They all listen and wait.

Fucking rotten little cunt. You can stay there and die. I'll lock the back door.

They all wait.

Joyce *goes back to the house.*

Angie *and* **Kit** *sit in silence for a while.*

Kit   When there's a war, where's the safest place?

Angie   Nowhere.

Kit   New Zealand is, my mum said. Your skin's burned right off. Shall we go to New Zealand?

Angie   I'm not staying here.

Kit   Shall we go to New Zealand?

Angie   You're not old enough.

Kit   You're not old enough.

Angie   I'm old enough to get married.

Kit   You don't want to get married.

Angie   No but I'm old enough.

Kit   I'd find out where they were going to drop it and stand right in the place.[26]

Angie   You couldn't find out.

---

26 Kit is talking about the threat of nuclear bombs.

Kit   Better than walking round with your skin dragging on the ground. Eugh. / Would you like walking round with your skin dragging on the ground?

Angie   You couldn't find out, stupid, it's a secret.

Kit   Where are you going?

Angie   I'm not telling you.

Kit   Why?

Angie   It's a secret.

Kit   But you tell me all your secrets.

Angie   Not the true secrets.

Kit   Yes you do.

Angie   No I don't.

Kit   I want to go somewhere away from the war.[27]

Angie   Just forget the war.

Kit   I can't.

Angie   You have to. It's so boring.

Kit   I'll remember it at night.

Angie   I'm going to do something else anyway.

Kit   What? Angie come on. Angie.

Angie   It's a true secret.

Kit   It can't be worse than the kitten. And killing your mother. And the war.

Angie   Well I'm not telling you so you can die for all I care.

---

27   Although it is possible that Kit is referring to the Falklands War, which occurred earlier the same year *Top Girls* was first produced, Kit's preoccupation with the threat of nuclear war means she is more likely referring to a second period of 'Cold War' style hostility between the Soviet Union and the West (particularly, the United States and Britain), which characterized the first half of the 1980s.

Kit   My mother says there's something wrong with you playing with someone my age. She says why haven't you got friends your own age. People your own age know there's something funny about you. She says you're a bad influence. She says she's going to speak to your mother.

Angie *twists* **Kit**'s *arm till she cries out.*

Angie   Say you're a liar.

Kit   She said it not me.

Angie   Say you eat shit.

Kit   You can't make me.

Angie *lets go.*

Angie   I don't care anyway. I'm leaving.

Kit   Go on then.

Angie   You'll all wake up one morning and find I've gone.

Kit   Good.

Angie   I'm not telling you when.

Kit   Go on then.

Angie   I'm sorry I hurt you.

Kit   I'm tired.

Angie   Do you like me?

Kit   I don't know.

Angie   You do like me.

Kit   I'm going home.

Kit *gets up.*

Angie   No you're not.

Kit   I'm tired.

Angie   She'll see you.

Kit   She'll give me a chocolate biscuit.

Angie   Kitty.

Kit   Tell me where you're going.

Angie   Sit down.

Kit *sits in the hut again.*

Kit   Go on then.

Angie   Swear?

Kit   Swear.

Angie   I'm going to London. To see my aunt.

Kit   And what?

Angie   That's it.

Kit   I see my aunt all the time.

Angie   I don't see my aunt.

Kit   What's so special?

Angie   It is special. She's special.

Kit   Why?

Angie   She is.

Kit   Why?

Angie   She is.

Kit   Why?

Angie   My mother hates her.

Kit   Why?

Angie   Because she does.

Kit   Perhaps she's not very nice.

Angie   She is nice.

Kit   How do you know?

Angie   Because I know her.

Kit   You said you never see her.

Angie   I saw her last year. You saw her.

Kit   Did I?

Angie   Never mind.

Kit   I remember her. That aunt. What's so special?

Angie   She gets people jobs.

Kit   What's so special?

Angie   I think I'm my aunt's child. I think my mother's really my aunt.

Kit   Why?

Angie   Because she goes to America, now shut up.

Kit   I've been to London.

Angie   Now give us a cuddle and shut up because I'm sick.

Kit   You're sitting on my arm.

Silence.

Joyce *comes out and comes up to them quietly.*

Joyce   Come on.

Kit   Oh hello.

Joyce   Time you went home.

Kit   We want to go to the Odeon.

Joyce   What time?

Kit   Don't know.

Joyce   What's on?

Kit   Don't know.

Joyce   Don't know much do you?

Kit   That all right then?

Joyce   Angie's got to clean her room first.

Angie   No I don't.

Joyce   Yes you do, it's a pigsty.

Angie   Well I'm not.

Joyce   Then you're not going. I don't care.

Angie   Well I am going.

Joyce   You've no money, have you?

Angie   Kit's paying anyway.

Joyce   No she's not.

Kit   I'll help you with your room.

Joyce   That's nice.

Angie   No you won't. You wait here.

Kit   Hurry then.

Angie   I'm not hurrying. You just wait.

Angie *goes into the house. Silence.*

Joyce   I don't know.

Silence.

How's school then?

Kit   All right.

Joyce   What are you now? Third year?

Kit   Second year.

Joyce   Your mum says you're good at English.

Silence.

Maybe Angie should've stayed on.

Kit   She didn't like it.

Joyce   I didn't like it. And look at me. If your face fits at school it's going to fit other places too. It wouldn't make no difference to Angie. She's not going to get a job when jobs are hard to get. I'd be sorry for anyone in charge of her. She'd better get married. I don't know who'd have her, mind. She's one of those girls might never leave home. What do you want to be when you grow up, Kit?

Kit   Physicist.

Joyce   What?

Kit   Nuclear physicist.

Joyce   Whatever for?

Kit   I could, I'm clever.

Joyce   I know you're clever, pet.

Silence.

I'll make a cup of tea.

Silence.

Looks like it's going to rain.

Silence.

Don't you have friends your own age?

Kit   Yes.

Joyce   Well then.

Kit   I'm old for my age.

Joyce   And Angie's simple is she? She's not simple.

Kit   I love Angie.

Joyce   She's clever in her own way.

Kit   You can't stop me.

Joyce   I don't want to.

Kit   You can't, so.

Joyce   Don't be cheeky, Kitty. She's always kind to little children.

Kit   She's coming so you better leave me alone.

Angie *comes out. She has changed into an old best dress, slightly small for her.*

Joyce   What you put that on for? Have you done your room? You can't clean your room in that.

Angie   I looked in the cupboard and it was there.

Joyce   Of course it was there, it's meant to be there. Is that why it was a surprise, finding something in the right place? I should think she's surprised, wouldn't you Kit, to find something in her room in the right place.

Angie   I decided to wear it.

Joyce   Not today, why? To clean your room? You're not going to the pictures till you've done your room. You can put your dress on after if you like.

Angie *picks up a brick.*

Have you done your room? You're not getting out of it, you know.

Kit   Angie, let's go.

Joyce   She's not going till she's done her room.

Kit   It's starting to rain.

Joyce   Come on, come on then. Hurry and do your room, Angie, and then you can go to the cinema with Kit. Oh it's wet, come on. We'll look up the time in the paper. Does your mother know, Kit, it's going to be a late night for you, isn't it? Hurry up, Angie. You'll spoil your dress. You make me sick.

Joyce *and* **Kit** *run in.*

Angie *stays where she is. Sound of rain.*

Kit *comes out of the house and shouts.*

Kit   Angie. Angie, come on, you'll get wet.

Kit *comes back to* **Angie**.

Angie   I put on this dress to kill my mother.

Kit   I suppose you thought you'd do it with a brick.

Angie   You can kill people with a brick.

Kit   Well you didn't, so.

Scene Two

Office of 'Top Girls' Employment Agency. Three desks and a small interviewing area. Monday morning. **Win** *and* **Nell** *have just arrived for work.*

Nell   Coffee coffee coffee coffee / coffee.

Win   The roses were smashing. / Mermaid.

Nell   Ohhh.

Win   Iceberg. He taught me all their names.

Nell *has some coffee now.*

Nell   Ah. Now then.

Win   He has one of the finest rose gardens in West Sussex. He exhibits.

Nell   He what?

Win   His wife was visiting her mother. It was like living together.

Nell   Crafty, you never said.

Win   He rang on Saturday morning.

Nell   Lucky you were free.

Win   That's what I told him.

Nell   Did you hell.

Win   Have you ever seen a really beautiful rose garden?

Nell   I don't like flowers. / I like swimming pools.

Win   Marilyn. Esther's Baby. They're all called after birds.[28]

Nell   Our friend's late. Celebrating all weekend I bet you.

Win   I'd call a rose Elvis. Or John Conteh.[29]

Nell   Is Howard in yet?

Win   If he is he'll be bleeping us with a problem.

Nell   Howard can just hang on to himself.

Win   Howard's really cut up.

Nell   Howard thinks because he's a fella the job was his as of right. Our Marlene's got far more balls than Howard and that's that.

Win   Poor little bugger.

Nell   He'll live.

Win   He'll move on.

Nell   I wouldn't mind a change of air myself.

Win   Serious?

Nell   I've never been a staying put lady. Pastures new.

Win   So who's the pirate?[30]

Nell   There's nothing definite.

Win   Inquiries?

Nell   There's always inquiries. I'd think I'd got bad breath if there stopped being inquiries. Most of them can't afford me. Or you.

---

28 Win means 'birds' as slang for 'women'.
29 A British light-heavyweight boxer, highly successful in the 1970s and popular long after.
30 By 'pirate', Win means a company or employer looking to steal Nell away from them.

Win   I'm all right for the time being. Unless I go to Australia.

Nell   There's not a lot of room upward.

Win   Marlene's filled it up.

Nell   Good luck to her. Unless there's some prospects moneywise.

Win   You can but ask.

Nell   Can always but ask.

Win   So what have we got? I've got a Mr Holden I saw last week.

Nell   Any use?

Win   Pushy. Bit of a cowboy.

Nell   Good-looker?

Win   Good dresser.

Nell   High flyer?

Win   That's his general idea certainly but I'm not sure he's got it up there.

Nell   Prestel wants six high flyers and I've only seen two and a half.[31]

Win   He's making a bomb on the road but he thinks it's time for an office. I sent him to IBM but he didn't get it.[32]

Nell   Prestel's on the road.

Win   He's not overbright.

Nell   Can he handle an office?

Win   Provided his secretary can punctuate he should go far.

---

31 At the time, Prestel were an up-and-coming information retrieval company, offering high-tech and desirable jobs.

32 The international technology company IBM would have been seen as another prestigious employer.

Nell   Bear Prestel in mind then, I might put my head round the door. I've got that poor little nerd I should never have said I could help. Tender heart me.

Win   Tender like old boots. How old?

Nell   Yes well forty-five.

Win   Say no more.

Nell   He knows his place, he's not after calling himself a manager, he's just a poor little bod wants a better commission and a bit of sunshine.

Win   Don't we all.

Nell   He's just got to relocate. He's got a bungalow in Dymchurch.

Win   And his wife says.

Nell   The lady wife wouldn't care to relocate. She's going through the change.[33]

Win   It's his funeral, don't waste your time.

Nell   I don't waste a lot.

Win   Good weekend you?

Nell   You could say.

Win   Which one?

Nell   One Friday, one Saturday.

Win   Aye aye.

Nell   Sunday night I watched telly.

Win   Which of them do you like best really?

Nell   Sunday was best, I liked the Ovaltine.

Win   Holden, Barker, Gardner, Duke.

---

33 An old-fashioned euphemism for the menopause.

Nell   I've a lady here thinks she can sell.

Win   Taking her on?

Nell   She's had some jobs.

Win   Services?

Nell   No, quite heavy stuff, electric.

Win   Tough bird like us.

Nell   We could do with a few more here.

Win   There's nothing going here.

Nell   No but I always want the tough ones when I see them. Hang on to them.

Win   I think we're plenty.

Nell   Derek asked me to marry him again.

Win   He doesn't know when he's beaten.

Nell   I told him I'm not going to play house, not even in Ascot.

Win   Mind you, you could play house.

Nell   If I chose to play house I would play house ace.

Win   You could marry him and go on working.

Nell   I could go on working and not marry him.

Marlene *arrives.*

Marlene   Morning ladies.

Win *and* **Nell** *cheer and whistle.*

Mind my head.

Nell   Coffee coffee coffee.

Win   We're tactfully not mentioning you're late.

Marlene   Fucking tube.

Win   We've heard that one.

Nell   We've used that one.

Win   It's the top executive doesn't come in as early as the poor working girl.

Marlene   Pass the sugar and shut your face, pet.

Win   Well I'm delighted.

Nell   Howard's looking sick.

Win   Howard is sick. He's got ulcers and heart. He told me.

Nell   He'll have to stop then won't he?

Win   Stop what?

Nell   Smoking, drinking, shouting. Working.

Win   Well, working.

Nell   We're just looking through the day.

Marlene   I'm doing some of Pam's ladies. They've been piling up while she's away.

Nell   Half a dozen little girls and an arts graduate who can't type.

Win   I spent the whole weekend at his place in Sussex.

Nell   She fancies his rose garden.

Win   I had to lie down in the back of the car so the neighbours wouldn't see me go in.

Nell   You're kidding.

Win   It was funny.

Nell   Fuck that for a joke.

Win   It was funny.

Marlene   Anyway they'd see you in the garden.

Win   The garden has extremely high walls.

Nell   I think I'll tell the wife.

Win   Like hell.

Nell   She might leave him and you could have the rose garden.

Win   The minute it's not a secret I'm out on my ear.

Nell   Don't know why you bother.

Win   Bit of fun.

Nell   I think it's time you went to Australia.

Win   I think it's pushy Mr Holden time.

Nell   If you've any really pretty bastards, Marlene, I want some for Prestel.

Marlene   I might have one this afternoon. This morning it's all Pam's secretarial.

Nell   Not long now and you'll be upstairs watching over us all.

Marlene   Do you feel bad about it?

Nell   I don't like coming second.

Marlene   Who does?

Win   We'd rather it was you than Howard. We're glad for you, aren't we Nell.

Nell   Oh yes. Aces.

Interview

Marlene *and* **Jeanine.**

Marlene   Right Jeanine, you are Jeanine aren't you? Let's have a look. Os and As.³⁴ / No As, all those Os you probably

Jeanine   Six Os.

34   Marlene is referring to 'A' levels and 'O' levels (the former name for GCSEs).

Marlene   could have got an A. / Speeds, not brilliant, not too bad.[35]

Jeanine   I wanted to go to work.

Marlene   Well, Jeanine, what's your present job like?

Jeanine   I'm a secretary.

Marlene   Secretary or typist?

Jeanine   I did start as a typist but the last six months I've been a secretary.

Marlene   To?

Jeanine   To three of them, really, they share me. There's Mr Ashford, he's the office manager, and Mr Philby / is sales, and –

Marlene   Quite a small place?

Jeanine   A bit small.

Marlene   Friendly?

Jeanine   Oh it's friendly enough.

Marlene   Prospects?

Jeanine   I don't think so, that's the trouble. Miss Lewis is secretary to the managing director and she's been there forever, and Mrs Bradford / is –

Marlene   So you want a job with better prospects?

Jeanine   I want a change.

Marlene   So you'll take anything comparable?

Jeanine   No, I do want prospects. I want more money.

Marlene   You're getting –?

Jeanine   Hundred.[36]

---

35   Marlene is referring to typing speeds (how many words you can type in a minute), an important skill for secretaries.

36   One hundred pounds a week salary: a decent wage for a young secretary at this time.

Marlene   It's not bad you know. You're what? Twenty?

Jeanine   I'm saving to get married.

Marlene   Does that mean you don't want a long-term job, Jeanine?

Jeanine   I might do.

Marlene   Because where do the prospects come in? No kids for a bit?

Jeanine   Oh no, not kids, not yet.

Marlene   So you won't tell them you're getting married?

Jeanine   Had I better not?

Marlene   It would probably help.

Jeanine   I'm not wearing a ring. We thought we wouldn't spend on a ring.

Marlene   Saves taking it off.

Jeanine   I wouldn't take it off.

Marlene   There's no need to mention it when you go for an interview. / Now Jeanine do you have a feel for any particular

Jeanine   But what if they ask?

Marlene   kind of company?

Jeanine   I thought advertising.

Marlene   People often do think advertising. I have got a few vacancies but I think they're looking for something glossier.

Jeanine   You mean how I dress? / I can dress different. I

Marlene   I mean experience.

Jeanine   dress like this on purpose for where I am now.

Marlene   I have a marketing department here of a knitwear manufacturer. / Marketing is near enough advertising. Secretary

Jeanine   Knitwear?

Marlene   to the marketing manager, he's thirty-five, married, I've sent him a girl before and she was happy, left to have a baby, you won't want to mention marriage there. He's very fair I think, good at his job, you won't have to nurse him along. Hundred and ten, so that's better than you're doing now.

Jeanine   I don't know.

Marlene   I've a fairly small concern here, father and two sons, you'd have more say potentially, secretarial and reception duties, only a hundred but the job's going to grow with the concern and then you'll be in at the top with new girls coming in underneath you.

Jeanine   What is it they do?

Marlene   Lampshades. / This would be my first choice for you.

Jeanine   Just lampshades?

Marlene   There's plenty of different kinds of lampshade. So we'll send you there, shall we, and the knitwear second choice. Are you free to go for an interview any day they call you?

Jeanine   I'd like to travel.

Marlene   We don't have any foreign clients. You'd have to go elsewhere.

Jeanine   Yes I know. I don't really . . . I just mean . . .

Marlene   Does your fiancé want to travel?

Jeanine   I'd like a job where I was here in London and with him and everything but now and then – I expect it's silly. Are there jobs like that?

Marlene   There's personal assistant to a top executive in a multinational. If that's the idea you need to be planning ahead. Is that where you want to be in ten years?

Jeanine   I might not be alive in ten years.

Marlene   Yes but you will be. You'll have children.

Jeanine   I can't think about ten years.

Marlene   You haven't got the speeds anyway. So I'll send you to these two shall I? You haven't been to any other agency? Just so we don't get crossed wires. Now Jeanine I want you to get one of these jobs, all right? If I send you that means I'm putting myself on the line for you. Your presentation's OK, you look fine, just be confident and go in there convinced that this is the best job for you and you're the best person for the job. If you don't believe it they won't believe it.

Jeanine   Do you believe it?

Marlene   I think you could make me believe it if you put your mind to it.

Jeanine   Yes, all right.

Interview

Win *and* **Louise**.

Win   Now Louise, hello, I have your details here. You've been very loyal to the one job I see.

Louise   Yes I have.

Win   Twenty-one years is a long time in one place.

Louise   I feel it is. I feel it's time to move on.

Win   And you are what age now?

Louise   I'm in my early forties.

Win   Exactly?

Louise   Forty-six.

Win   It's not necessarily a handicap, well it is of course we have to face that, but it's not necessarily a disabling handicap, experience does count for something.

Louise   I hope so.

Win   Now between ourselves is there any trouble, any reason why you're leaving that wouldn't appear on the form?

Louise   Nothing like that.

Win   Like what?

Louise   Nothing at all.

Win   No long-term understandings come to a sudden end, making for an insupportable atmosphere?

Louise   I've always completely avoided anything like that at all.

Win   No personality clashes with your immediate superiors or inferiors?

Louise   I've always taken care to get on very well with everyone.

Win   I only ask because it can affect the reference and it also affects your motivation, I want to be quite clear why you're moving on. So I take it the job itself no longer satisfies you. Is it the money?

Louise   It's partly the money. It's not so much the money.

Win   Nine thousand is very respectable. Have you dependants?

Louise   No, no dependants. My mother died.

Win   So why are you making a change?

Louise   Other people make changes.

Win   But why are you, now, after spending most of your life in the one place?

Louise   There you are, I've lived for that company, I've given my life really you could say because I haven't had a great deal of social life, I've worked in the evenings. I haven't had office entanglements for the very reason you just mentioned and if you are committed to your work you don't move in many other circles. I had management status from the age of twenty-seven and you'll appreciate what that means. I've built up a department. And there it is, it works extremely well, and I feel I'm stuck there. I've spent twenty years in middle management. I've seen young men who I trained go on, in my own company or elsewhere, to higher things. Nobody notices me, I don't expect it, I don't attract attention by making mistakes, everybody takes it for granted that my work is perfect. They will notice me when I go, they will be sorry I think to lose me, they will offer me more money of course, I will refuse. They will see when I've gone what I was doing for them.

Win   If they offer you more money you won't stay?

Louise   No I won't.

Win   Are you the only woman?

Louise   Apart from the girls of course, yes. There was one, she was my assistant, it was the only time I took on a young woman assistant, I always had my doubts. I don't care greatly for working with women, I think I pass as a man at work. But I did take on this young woman, her qualifications were excellent, and she did well, she got a department of her own, and left the company for a competitor where she's now on the board and good luck to her. She has a different style, she's a new kind of attractive well-dressed – I don't mean I don't dress properly. But there is a kind of woman who is thirty now who grew up in a different climate. They are not so careful. They take themselves for granted. I have had to justify my existence every minute, and I have done so, I have proved – well.

Win   Let's face it, vacancies are going to be ones where you'll be in competition with younger men. And there are companies that will value your experience enough you'll be in with a chance. There are also fields that are easier for a woman, there is a cosmetic company here where your experience might be relevant. It's eight and a half, I don't know if that appeals.

Louise   I've proved I can earn money. It's more important to get away. I feel it's now or never. I sometimes / think –

Win   You shouldn't talk too much at an interview.

Louise   I don't. I don't normally talk about myself. I know very well how to handle myself in an office situation. I only talk to you because it seems to me this is different, it's your job to understand me, surely. You asked the questions.

Win   I think I understand you sufficiently.

Louise   Well good, that's good.

Win   Do you drink?

Louise   Certainly not. I'm not a teetotaller, I think that's very suspect, it's seen as being an alcoholic if you're teetotal. What do you mean? I don't drink. Why?

Win   I drink.

Louise   I don't.

Win   Good for you.

Main office

Marlene *and* **Angie.**

Angie *arrives.*

Angie   Hello.

Marlene   Have you an appointment?

Angie   It's me. I've come.

Marlene   What? It's not Angie?

Angie   It was hard to find this place. I got lost.

Marlene   How did you get past the receptionist? The girl on the desk, didn't she try to stop you?

Angie   What desk?

Marlene   Never mind.

Angie   I just walked in. I was looking for you.

Marlene   Well you found me.

Angie   Yes.

Marlene   So where's your mum? Are you up in town for the day?

Angie   Not really.

Marlene   Sit down. Do you feel all right?

Angie   Yes thank you.

Marlene   So where's Joyce?

Angie   She's at home.

Marlene   Did you come up on a school trip then?

Angie   I've left school.

Marlene   Did you come up with a friend?

Angie   No. There's just me.

Marlene   You came up by yourself, that's fun. What have you been doing? Shopping? Tower of London?

Angie   No, I just come here. I come to you.

Marlene   That's very nice of you to think of paying your aunty a visit. There's not many nieces make that the first port of call. Would you like a cup of coffee?

Angie   No thank you.

Marlene   Tea, orange?

Angie   No thank you.

Marlene   Do you feel all right?

Angie   Yes thank you.

Marlene   Are you tired from the journey?

Angie   Yes, I'm tired from the journey.

Marlene   You sit there for a bit then. How's Joyce?

Angie   She's all right.

Marlene   Same as ever.

Angie   Oh yes.

Marlene   Unfortunately you've picked a day when I'm rather busy, if there's ever a day when I'm not, or I'd take you out to lunch and we'd go to Madame Tussaud's. We could go shopping. What time do you have to be back? Have you got a day return?

Angie   No.

Marlene   So what train are you going back on?

Angie   I came on the bus.

Marlene   So what bus are you going back on? Are you staying the night?

Angie   Yes.

Marlene   Who are you staying with? Do you want me to put you up for the night, is that it?

Angie   Yes please.

Marlene   I haven't got a spare bed.

Angie   I can sleep on the floor.

Marlene   You can sleep on the sofa.

Angie   Yes please.

Marlene   I do think Joyce might have phoned me. It's like her.

Angie   This is where you work is it?

Marlene   It's where I have been working the last two years but I'm going to move into another office.

Angie   It's lovely.

Marlene   My new office is nicer than this. There's just the one big desk in it for me.

Angie   Can I see it?

Marlene   Not now, no, there's someone else in it now. But he's leaving at the end of next week and I'm going to do his job.

Angie   Is that good?

Marlene   Yes, it's very good.

Angie   Are you going to be in charge?

Marlene   Yes I am.

Angie   I knew you would be.

Marlene   How did you know?

Angie   I knew you'd be in charge of everything.

Marlene   Not quite everything.

Angie   You will be.

Marlene   Well we'll see.

Angie   Can I see it next week then?

Marlene   Will you still be here next week?

Angie   Yes.

Marlene   Don't you have to go home?

Angie   No.

Marlene   Why not?

Angie   It's all right.

Marlene   Is it all right?

Angie   Yes, don't worry about it.

Marlene   Does Joyce know where you are?

Angie   Yes of course she does.

Marlene   Well does she?

Angie   Don't worry about it.

Marlene   How long are you planning to stay with me then?

Angie   You know when you came to see us last year?

Marlene   Yes, that was nice wasn't it?

Angie   That was the best day of my whole life.

Marlene   So how long are you planning to stay?

Angie   Don't you want me?

Marlene   Yes yes, I just wondered.

Angie   I won't stay if you don't want me.

Marlene   No, of course you can stay.

Angie   I'll sleep on the floor. I won't be any bother.

Marlene   Don't get upset.

Angie   I'm not, I'm not. Don't worry about it.

Mrs Kidd *comes in.*

Mrs Kidd   Excuse me.

Marlene   Yes.

Mrs Kidd   Excuse me.

Marlene   Can I help you?

Mrs Kidd   Excuse me bursting in on you like this but I have to talk to you.

Marlene   I am engaged at the moment. / If you could go to reception –

Mrs Kidd   I'm Rosemary Kidd, Howard's wife, you don't recognise me but we did meet, I remember you of course / but you wouldn't –

Marlene   Yes of course, Mrs Kidd, I'm sorry, we did meet. Howard's about somewhere I expect, have you looked in his office?

Mrs Kidd   Howard's not about, no. I'm afraid it's you I've come to see if I could have a minute or two.

Marlene   I do have an appointment in five minutes.

Mrs Kidd   This won't take five minutes. I'm very sorry. It is a matter of some urgency.

Marlene   Well of course. What can I do for you?

Mrs Kidd   I just wanted a chat, an informal chat. It's not something I can simply – I'm sorry if I'm interrupting your work. I know office work isn't like housework / which is all interruptions.

Marlene   No no, this is my niece, Angie. Mrs Kidd.

Mrs Kidd   Very pleased to meet you.

Angie   Very well thank you.

Mrs Kidd   Howard's not in today.

Marlene   Isn't he?

Mrs Kidd   He's feeling poorly.

Marlene   I didn't know. I'm sorry to hear that.

Mrs Kidd   The fact is he's in a state of shock. About what's happened.

Marlene   What has happened?

Mrs Kidd   You should know if anyone. I'm referring to you being appointed managing director instead of Howard. He hasn't been at all well all weekend. He hasn't slept for three nights. I haven't slept.

Marlene   I'm sorry to hear that, Mrs Kidd. Has he thought of taking sleeping pills?

Mrs Kidd   It's very hard when someone has worked all these years.

Marlene   Business life is full of little setbacks. I'm sure Howard knows that. He'll bounce back in a day or two. We all bounce back.

Mrs Kidd   If you could see him you'd know what I'm talking about. What's it going to do to him working for a woman? I think if it was a man he'd get over it as something normal.

Marlene   I think he's going to have to get over it.

Mrs Kidd   It's me that bears the brunt. I'm not the one that's been promoted. I put him first every inch of the way. And now what do I get? You women this, you women that. It's not my fault. You're going to have to be very careful how you handle him. He's very hurt.

Marlene   Naturally I'll be tactful and pleasant to him, you don't start pushing someone round. I'll consult him over any decisions affecting his department. But that's no different, Mrs Kidd, from any of my other colleagues.

Mrs Kidd   I think it is different, because he's a man.

Marlene   I'm not quite sure why you came to see me.

Mrs Kidd   I had to do something.

Marlene   Well you've done it, you've seen me. I think that's probably all we've time for. I'm sorry he's been taking it out on you. He really is a shit, Howard.

Mrs Kidd   But he's got a family to support. He's got three children. It's only fair.

Marlene   Are you suggesting I give up the job to him then?

Mrs Kidd   It had crossed my mind if you were unavailable after all for some reason, he would be the natural second choice I think, don't you? I'm not asking.

Marlene   Good.

Mrs Kidd   You mustn't tell him I came. He's very proud.

Marlene   If he doesn't like what's happening here he can go and work somewhere else.

Mrs Kidd   Is that a threat?

Marlene   I'm sorry but I do have some work to do.

Mrs Kidd   It's not that easy, a man of Howard's age. You don't care. I thought he was going too far but he's right. You're one of these ballbreakers / that's what you are. You'll end up

Marlene   I'm sorry but I do have some work to do.

Mrs Kidd   miserable and lonely. You're not natural.

Marlene   Could you please piss off?

Mrs Kidd   I thought if I saw you at least I'd be doing something.

Mrs Kidd *goes.*

Marlene   I've got to go and do some work now. Will you come back later?

Angie   I think you were wonderful.

Marlene   I've got to go and do some work now.

Angie   You told her to piss off.

Marlene   Will you come back later?

Angie   Can't I stay here?

Marlene   Don't you want to go sightseeing?

Angie   I'd rather stay here.

Marlene   You can stay here I suppose, if it's not boring.

Angie   It's where I most want to be in the world.

Marlene   I'll see you later then.

Marlene *goes.*

Angie *sits at* **Win**'s *desk.*

Interview

Nell *and* **Shona**.

Nell   Is this right? You are Shona?

Shona   Yeh.

Nell   It says here you're twenty-nine.

Shona   Yeh.

Nell Too many late nights, me. So you've been where you are for four years, Shona, you're earning six basic and three commission.[37] So what's the problem?

Shona No problem.

Nell Why do you want a change?

Shona Just a change.

Nell Change of product, change of area?

Shona Both.

Nell But you're happy on the road?

Shona I like driving.

Nell You're not after management status?

Shona I would like management status.

Nell You'd be interested in titular management status but not come off the road?

Shona I want to be on the road, yeh.

Nell So how many calls have you been making a day?

Shona Six.

Nell And what proportion of those are successful?

Shona Six.

Nell That's hard to believe.

Shona Four.

Nell You find it easy to get the initial interest do you?

Shona Oh yeh, I get plenty of initial interest.

Nell And what about closing?[38]

---

37 Six thousand pounds a year as a salary, supplemented with another three thousand pounds for good performance/meeting sales targets.
38 Finalizing the deal/sale.

Shona   I close, don't I?

Nell   Because that's what an employer is going to have doubts about with a lady as I needn't tell you, whether she's got the guts to push through to a closing situation. They think we're too nice. They think we listen to the buyer's doubts. They think we consider his needs and his feelings.

Shona   I never consider people's feelings.

Nell   I was selling for six years, I can sell anything, I've sold in three continents, and I'm jolly as they come but I'm not very nice.

Shona   I'm not very nice.

Nell   What sort of time do you have on the road with the other reps? Get on all right? Handle the chat?

Shona   I get on. Keep myself to myself.

Nell   Fairly much of a loner are you?

Shona   Sometimes.

Nell   So what field are you interested in?

Shona   Computers.

Nell   That's a top field as you know and you'll be up against some very slick fellas there, there's some very pretty boys in computers, it's an American-style field.

Shona   That's why I want to do it.

Nell   Video systems appeal? That's a high-flying situation.

Shona   Video systems appeal OK.

Nell   Because Prestel have half a dozen vacancies I'm looking to fill at the moment. We're talking in the area of ten to fifteen thousand here and upwards.

Shona   Sounds OK.

Nell   I've half a mind to go for it myself. But it's good money here if you've got the top clients. Could you fancy it do you think?

Shona   Work here?

Nell   I'm not in a position to offer, there's nothing officially going just now, but we're always on the lookout. There's not that many of us. We could keep in touch.

Shona   I like driving.

Nell   So the Prestel appeals?

Shona   Yeh.

Nell   What about ties?

Shona   No ties.

Nell   So relocation wouldn't be a problem.

Shona   No problem.

Nell   So just fill me in a bit more could you about what you've been doing.

Shona   What I've been doing. It's all down there.

Nell   The bare facts are down here but I've got to present you to an employer.

Shona   I'm twenty-nine years old.

Nell   So it says here.

Shona   We look young. Youngness runs in the family in our family.

Nell   So just describe your present job for me.

Shona   My present job at present. I have a car. I have a Porsche. I go up the M1 a lot. Burn up the M1 a lot. Straight up the M1 in the fast lane to where the clients are, Staffordshire, Yorkshire, I do a lot in Yorkshire. I'm selling electric things. Like dishwashers, washing machines, stainless steel tubs are a feature and the reliability of the programme. After sales service, we offer a very good after sales service, spare parts, plenty of spare parts. And fridges, I sell a lot of fridges specially in the summer. People want to buy fridges in the summer because of the heat melting the butter and you get fed up standing the milk in a basin of cold water with a cloth over, stands to reason people don't want to do that in this day and age. So I sell a lot of them. Big ones with big freezers. Big freezers. And I stay in hotels at night when I'm away from home. On my expense account. I stay in various hotels. They know me, the ones I go to. I check in, have a bath, have a shower. Then I go down to the bar, have a gin and tonic, have a chat. Then I go into the dining room and have dinner. I usually have fillet steak and mushrooms, I like mushrooms. I like smoked salmon very much. I like having a salad on the side. Green salad. I don't like tomatoes.

Nell   Christ what a waste of time.

Shona   Beg your pardon?

Nell   Not a word of this is true is it?

Shona   How do you mean?

Nell   You just filled in the form with a pack of lies.

Shona   Not exactly.

Nell   How old are you?

Shona   Twenty-nine.

Nell   Nineteen?

Shona   Twenty-one.

Nell   And what jobs have you done? Have you done any?

Shona   I could though, I bet you.

Main office

Angie *sitting as before.*

Win *comes in.*

Win   Who's sitting in my chair?

Angie   What? Sorry.

Win   Who's been eating my porridge?

Angie What?

Win It's all right, I saw Marlene. Angie isn't it? I'm Win. And I'm not going out for lunch because I'm knackered. I'm going to set me down here and have a yoghurt. Do you like yoghurt?

Angie No.

Win That's good because I've only got one. Are you hungry?

Angie No.

Win There's a cafe on the corner.

Angie No thank you. Do you work here?

Win How did you guess?

Angie Because you look as if you might work here and you're sitting at the desk. Have you always worked here?

Win No I was headhunted. That means I was working for another outfit like this and this lot came and offered me more money. I broke my contract, there was a hell of a stink. There's not many top ladies about. Your aunty's a smashing bird.

Angie Yes I know.

Win Fan are you? Fan of your aunty's?

Angie Do you think I could work here?

Win Not at the moment.

Angie How do I start?

Win What can you do?

Angie I don't know. Nothing.

Win Type?

Angie Not very well. The letters jump up when I do capitals. I was going to do a CSE in commerce but I didn't.[39]

---

39 A CSE is a Certificate of Secondary Education: a former qualification offered in academic and vocational subjects, pitched and assessed at a lower level than an 'O' level.

Win   What have you got?

Angie   What?

Win   CSEs, Os.

Angie   Nothing, none of that. Did you do all that?

Win   Oh yes, all that, and a science degree funnily enough. I started out doing medical research but there's no money in it. I thought I'd go abroad. Did you know they sell Coca-Cola in Russia and Pepsi-cola in China? You don't have to be qualified as much as you might think. Men are awful bullshitters, they like to make out jobs are harder than they are. Any job I ever did I started doing it better than the rest of the crowd and they didn't like it. So I'd get unpopular and I'd have a drink to cheer myself up. I lived with a fella and supported him for four years, he couldn't get work. After that I went to California. I like the sunshine. Americans know how to live. This country's too slow. Then I went to Mexico, still in sales, but it's no country for a single lady. I came home, went bonkers for a bit, thought I was five different people, got over that all right, the psychiatrist said I was perfectly sane and highly intelligent. Got married in a moment of weakness and he's inside now, he's been inside four years, and I've not been to see him too much this last year. I like this better than sales, I'm not really that aggressive. I started thinking sales was a good job if you want to meet people, but you're meeting people that don't want to meet you. It's no good if you like being liked. Here your clients want to meet you because you're the one doing them some good. They hope.

Angie *has fallen asleep.* **Nell** *comes in.*

Nell   You're talking to yourself, sunshine.

Win   So what's new?

Nell   Who is this?

Win   Marlene's little niece.

Nell   What's she got, brother, sister? She never talks about her family.

Win I was telling her my life story.

Nell Violins?[40]

Win No, success story.

Nell You've heard Howard's had a heart attack?

Win No, when?

Nell I heard just now. He hadn't come in, he was at home, he's gone to hospital. He's not dead. His wife was here, she rushed off in a cab.

Win Too much butter, too much smoke. We must send him some flowers.

Marlene *comes in.*

You've heard about Howard?

Marlene Poor sod.

Nell Lucky he didn't get the job if that's what his health's like.

Marlene Is she asleep?

Win She wants to work here.

Marlene Packer in Tesco more like.

Win She's a nice kid. Isn't she?

Marlene She's a bit thick. She's a bit funny.

Win She thinks you're wonderful.

Marlene She's not going to make it.

---

40 A reference to playing poignant violin music over a sad story (for example, in a film soundtrack).

Act Three

A year earlier. Sunday evening. **Joyce**'s *kitchen.* **Joyce, Angie, Marlene. Marlene** *is taking presents out of a bright carrier bag.* **Angie** *has already opened a box of chocolates.*

Marlene   Just a few little things. / I've no memory for

Joyce   There's no need.

Marlene   birthdays have I, and Christmas seems to slip by. So I think I owe Angie a few presents.

Joyce   What do you say?

Angie   Thank you very much. Thank you very much, Aunty Marlene.

She opens a present. It is the dress from Act Two, new.

Angie   Oh look, Mum, isn't it lovely?

Marlene   I don't know if it's the right size. She's grown up since I saw her. / I knew she was always tall for her age.

Angie   Isn't it lovely?

Joyce   She's a big lump.

Marlene   Hold it up, Angie, let's see.

Angie   I'll put it on, shall I?

Marlene   Yes, try it on.

Joyce   Go on to your room then, we don't want / a strip show thank you.

Angie   Of course I'm going to my room, what do you think? Look Mum, here's something for you. Open it, go on. What is it? Can I open it for you?

Joyce   Yes, you open it, pet.

Angie   Don't you want to open it yourself? / Go on.

Joyce   I don't mind, you can do it.

Angie   It's something hard. It's – what is it? A bottle. Drink is it? No, it's what? Perfume, look. What a lot. Open it, look, let's smell it. Oh it's strong. It's lovely. Put it on me. How do you do it? Put it on me.

Joyce   You're too young.

Angie   I can play wearing it like dressing up.

Joyce   And you're too old for that. Here, give it here, I'll do it, you'll tip the whole bottle over yourself / and we'll have you smelling all summer.

Angie   Put it on you. Do I smell? Put it on Aunty too. Put it on Aunty too. Let's all smell.

Marlene   I didn't know what you'd like.

Joyce   There's no danger I'd have it already, / that's one thing.

Angie   Now we all smell the same.

Marlene   It's a bit of nonsense.

Joyce   It's very kind of you Marlene, you shouldn't.

Angie   Now. I'll put on the dress and then we'll see.

Angie *goes.*

Joyce   You've caught me on the hop with the place in a mess. / If you'd let me know you was coming I'd have got

Marlene   That doesn't matter.

Joyce   something in to eat. We had our dinner dinnertime. We're just going to have a cup of tea. You could have an egg.

Marlene   No, I'm not hungry. Tea's fine.

Joyce   I don't expect you take sugar.

Marlene   Why not?

Joyce   You take care of yourself.

Marlene   How do you mean you didn't know I was coming?

Joyce You could have written. I know we're not on the phone but we're not completely in the dark ages, / we do have a postman.[41]

Marlene But you asked me to come.

Joyce How did I ask you to come?

Marlene Angie said when she phoned up.

Joyce Angie phoned up, did she?

Marlene Was it just Angie's idea?

Joyce What did she say?

Marlene She said you wanted me to come and see you. / It was a couple of weeks ago. How was I to know that's a

Joyce Ha.

Marlene ridiculous idea? My diary's always full a couple of weeks ahead so we fixed it for this weekend. I was meant to get here earlier but I was held up. She gave me messages from you.

Joyce Didn't you wonder why I didn't phone you myself?

Marlene She said you didn't like using the phone. You're shy on the phone and can't use it. I don't know what you're like, do I.

Joyce Are there people who can't use the phone?

Marlene I expect so.

Joyce I haven't met any.

Marlene Why should I think she was lying?

Joyce Because she's like what she's like.

Marlene How do I know / what she's like?

Joyce It's not my fault you don't know what she's like. You never come and see her.

---

41 At the time the play was written, many people, particularly in the types of close-knit, working class community in which Joyce lives, did not have a phone in their own home, and would only be able to make calls from public phone boxes.

Marlene   Well I have now / and you don't seem over the moon.*

Joyce   Good.

*Well I'd have got a cake if she'd told me.

Pause.

Marlene   I did wonder why you wanted to see me.

Joyce   I didn't want to see you.

Marlene   Yes, I know. Shall I go?

Joyce   I don't mind seeing you.

Marlene   Great, I feel really welcome.

Joyce   You can come and see Angie any time you like, I'm not stopping you. / You know where we are. You're the

Marlene   Ta ever so.

Joyce   one went away, not me. I'm right here where I was.

And will be a few years yet I shouldn't wonder.

Marlene   All right. All right.

Joyce *gives* **Marlene** *a cup of tea.*

Joyce   Tea.

Marlene   Sugar?

Joyce *passes* **Marlene** *the sugar.*

It's very quiet down here.

Joyce   I expect you'd notice it.

Marlene   The air smells different too.

Joyce   That's the scent.

Marlene   No, I mean walking down the lane.

Joyce   What sort of air you get in London then?

Angie *comes in, wearing the dress. It fits.*

Marlene   Oh, very pretty. You do look pretty, Angie.

Joyce   That fits all right.

Marlene   Do you like the colour?

Angie   Beautiful. Beautiful.

Joyce   You better take it off, you'll get it dirty.

Angie   I want to wear it. I want to wear it.

Marlene   It is for wearing after all. You can't just hang it up and look at it.

Angie   I love it.

Joyce   Well if you must you must.

Angie   If someone asks me what's my favourite colour I'll tell them it's this. Thank you very much, Aunty Marlene.

Marlene   You didn't tell your mum you asked me down.

Angie   I wanted it to be a surprise.

Joyce   I'll give you a surprise / one of these days.

Angie   I thought you'd like to see her. She hasn't been here since I was nine. People do see their aunts.

Marlene   Is it that long? Doesn't time fly?

Angie   I wanted to.

Joyce   I'm not cross.

Angie   Are you glad?

Joyce   I smell nicer anyhow, don't I?

Kit *comes in without saying anything, as if she lived there.*

Marlene   I think it was a good idea, Angie, about time. We are sisters after all. It's a pity to let that go.

Joyce   This is Kitty, / who lives up the road. This is Angie's Aunty Marlene.

Kit   What's that?

Angie   It's a present. Do you like it?

Kit   It's all right. / Are you coming out?

Marlene   Hello, Kitty.

Angie   *No.

Kit   What's that smell?

Angie   It's a present.

Kit   It's horrible. Come on.

Marlene   Have a chocolate.

Angie   *No, I'm busy.

Kit   Coming out later?

Angie   No.

Kit (*to* **Marlene**)   Hello.

Kit *goes without a chocolate.*

Joyce   She's a little girl Angie sometimes plays with because she's the only child lives really close. She's like a little sister to her really. Angie's good with little children.

Marlene   Do you want to work with children, Angie? / Be a teacher or a nursery nurse?

Joyce   I don't think she's ever thought of it.

Marlene   What do you want to do?

Joyce   She hasn't an idea in her head what she wants to do. / Lucky to get anything.

Marlene   Angie?

Joyce   She's not clever like you.

Pause.

Marlene   I'm not clever, just pushy.

Joyce   True enough.

Marlene *takes a bottle of whisky out of the bag.*

I don't drink spirits.

Angie   You do at Christmas.

Joyce   It's not Christmas, is it?

Angie   It's better than Christmas.

Marlene   Glasses?

Joyce   Just a small one then.

Marlene   Do you want some, Angie?

Angie   I can't, can I?

Joyce   Taste it if you want. You won't like it.

Marlene   We got drunk together the night your grandfather died.

Joyce   We did not get drunk.

Marlene   I got drunk. You were just overcome with grief.

Joyce   I still keep up the grave with flowers.

Marlene   Do you really?

Joyce   Why wouldn't I?

Marlene   Have you seen Mother?

Joyce   Of course I've seen Mother.

Marlene   I mean lately.

Joyce   Of course I've seen her lately, I go every Thursday.

Marlene (*to* **Angie**)   Do you remember your grandfather?

Angie   He got me out of the bath one night in a towel.

Marlene   Did he? I don't think he ever gave me a bath. Did he give you a bath, Joyce? He probably got soft in his old age. Did you like him?

Angie   Yes of course.

Marlene   Why?

Angie   What?

Marlene   So what's the news? How's Mrs Paisley? Still going crazily? / And Dorothy. What happened to Dorothy?*

Angie   Who's Mrs Paisley?

Joyce   *She went to Canada.

Marlene   Did she? What to do?

Joyce   I don't know. She just went to Canada.

Marlene   Well / good for her.

Angie   Mr Connolly killed his wife.

Marlene   What, Connolly at Whitegates?

Angie   They found her body in the garden. / Under the cabbages.

Marlene   He was always so proper.

Joyce   Stuck up git. Connolly. Best lawyer money could buy but he couldn't get out of it. She was carrying on with Matthew.

Marlene   How old's Matthew then?

Joyce   Twenty-one. / He's got a motorbike.

Marlene   I think he's about six.

Angie   How can he be six? He's six years older than me. / If he was six I'd be nothing, I'd be just born this minute.

Joyce   Your aunty knows that, she's just being silly. She means it's so long since she's been here she's forgotten about Matthew.

Angie   You were here for my birthday when I was nine. I had a pink cake. Kit was only five then, she was four, she hadn't started school yet. She could read already when she went to school. You remember my birthday? / You remember me?

Marlene   Yes, I remember the cake.

Angie   You remember me?

Marlene   Yes, I remember you.

Angie   And Mum and Dad was there, and Kit was.

Marlene   Yes, how is your dad? Where is he tonight? Up the pub?

Joyce   No, he's not here.

Marlene   I can see he's not here.

Joyce   He moved out.

Marlene   What? When did he? /Just recently?*

Angie   Didn't you know that? You don't know much.

Joyce   *No, it must be three years ago. Don't be rude, Angie.

Angie   I'm not, am I Aunty? What else don't you know?

Joyce   You was in America or somewhere. You sent a postcard.

Angie   I've got that in my room. It's the Grand Canyon. Do you want to see it? Shall I get it? I can get it for you.

Marlene   Yes, all right.

Angie *goes.*

Joyce   You could be married with twins for all I know. You must have affairs and break up and I don't need to know about any of that so I don't see what the fuss is about.

Marlene   What fuss?

Angie *comes back with the postcard.*

Angie   'Driving across the states for a new job in L.A. It's a long way but the car goes very fast. It's very hot. Wish you were here. Love from Aunty Marlene.'

Joyce   Did you make a lot of money?

Marlene   I spent a lot.

Angie   I want to go to America. Will you take me?

Joyce   She's not going to America, she's been to America, stupid.

Angie   She might go again, stupid. It's not something you do once. People who go keep going all the time, back and forth on jets. They go on Concorde and Laker and get jet lag. Will you take me?

Marlene   I'm not planning a trip.

Angie   Will you let me know?

Joyce   Angie, / you're getting silly.

Angie   I want to be American.

Joyce   It's time you were in bed.

Angie   No it's not. / I don't have to go to bed at all tonight.

Joyce   School in the morning.

Angie   I'll wake up.

Joyce   Come on now, you know how you get.

Angie   How do I get? / I don't get anyhow.

Joyce   Angie. Are you staying the night?

Marlene   Yes, if that's all right. / I'll see you in the morning.

Angie   You can have my bed. I'll sleep on the sofa.

Joyce   You will not, you'll sleep in your bed. / Think I can't

Angie   Mum.

Joyce   see through that? I can just see you going to sleep / with us talking.

Angie   I would, I would go to sleep, I'd love that.

Joyce   I'm going to get cross, Angie.

Angie   I want to show her something.

Joyce   Then bed.

Angie   It's a secret.

Joyce   Then I expect it's in your room so off you go. Give us a shout when you're ready for bed and your aunty'll be up and see you.

Angie   Will you?

Marlene   Yes of course.

Angie *goes.*

Silence.

It's cold tonight.

Joyce   Will you be all right on the sofa? You can / have my bed.

Marlene   The sofa's fine.

Joyce   Yes the forecast said rain tonight but it's held off.

Marlene   I was going to walk down to the estuary but I've left it a bit late. Is it just the same?

Joyce   They cut down the hedges a few years back. Is that since you were here?

Marlene   But it's not changed down the end, all the mud? And the reeds? We used to pick them when they were bigger than us. Are there still lapwings?

Joyce   You get strangers walking there on a Sunday. I expect they're looking at the mud and the lapwings, yes.

Marlene   You could have left.

Joyce   Who says I wanted to leave?

Marlene   Stop getting at me then, you're really boring.

Joyce   How could I have left?

Marlene   Did you want to?

Joyce   I said how, / how could I?

Marlene   If you'd wanted to you'd have done it.

Joyce   Christ.

Marlene   Are we getting drunk?

Joyce   Do you want something to eat?

Marlene   No, I'm getting drunk.

Joyce   Funny time to visit, Sunday evening.

Marlene   I came this morning. I spent the day.

Angie (*off*)   Aunty! Aunty Marlene!

Marlene   I'd better go.

Joyce   Go on then.

Marlene   All right.

Angie (*off*)   Aunty! Can you hear me? I'm ready.

Marlene *goes.*

Joyce *goes on sitting.*

Marlene *comes back.*

Joyce   So what's the secret?

Marlene   It's a secret.

Joyce   I know what it is anyway.

Marlene   I bet you don't. You always said that.

Joyce   It's her exercise book.

Marlene   Yes, but you don't know what's in it.

Joyce   It's some game, some secret society she has with Kit.

Marlene   You don't know the password. You don't know the code.

Joyce   You're really in it, aren't you. Can you do the handshake?

Marlene   She didn't mention a handshake.

Joyce   I thought they'd have a special handshake. She spends hours writing that but she's useless at school. She copies things out of books about black magic, and politicians out of the paper. It's a bit childish.

Marlene   I think it's a plot to take over the world.

Joyce   She's been in the remedial class the last two years.

Marlene   I came up this morning and spent the day in Ipswich. I went to see Mother.

Joyce   Did she recognise you?

Marlene   Are you trying to be funny?

Joyce   No, she does wander.

Marlene   She wasn't wandering at all, she was very lucid thank you.

Joyce   You were very lucky then.

Marlene   Fucking awful life she's had.

Joyce   Don't tell me.

Marlene   Fucking waste.

Joyce   Don't talk to me.

Marlene   Why shouldn't I talk? Why shouldn't I talk to you? / Isn't she my mother too?

Joyce   Look, you've left, you've gone away, / we can do without you.

Marlene   I left home, so what, I left home. People do leave home / it is normal.

Joyce   We understand that, we can do without you.

Marlene   We weren't happy. Were you happy?

Joyce   Don't come back.

Marlene   So it's just your mother is it, your child, you never wanted me round, / you were jealous of me because I was the

Joyce   Here we go.

Marlene   little one and I was clever.

Joyce   I'm not clever enough for all this psychology / if that's what it is.

Marlene   Why can't I visit my own family / without all this?*

Joyce Aah.

Just don't go on about Mum's life when you haven't been to see her for how many years. / I go and see her every week.

Marlene It's up to me.

*Then don't go and see her every week.

Joyce Somebody has to.

Marlene No they don't. / Why do they?

Joyce How would I feel if I didn't go?

Marlene A lot better.

Joyce I hope you feel better.

Marlene It's up to me.

Joyce You couldn't get out of here fast enough.

Marlene Of course I couldn't get out of here fast enough. What was I going to do? Marry a dairyman who'd come home pissed? / Don't you fucking this fucking that fucking bitch

Joyce Christ.

Marlene fucking tell me what to fucking do fucking.

Joyce I don't know how you could leave your own child.

Marlene You were quick enough to take her.

Joyce What does that mean?

Marlene You were quick enough to take her.

Joyce Or what? Have her put in a home? Have some stranger / take her would you rather?

Marlene You couldn't have one so you took mine.

Joyce I didn't know that then.

Marlene Like hell, / married three years.

Joyce I didn't know that. Plenty of people / take that long.

Marlene Well it turned out lucky for you, didn't it?

Joyce   Turned out all right for you by the look of you. You'd be getting a few less thousand a year.

Marlene   Not necessarily.

Joyce   You'd be stuck here / like you said.

Marlene   I could have taken her with me.

Joyce   You didn't want to take her with you. It's no good coming back now, Marlene, / and saying –

Marlene   I know a managing director who's got two children, she breast feeds in the board room, she pays a hundred pounds a week on domestic help alone and she can afford that because she's an extremely high-powered lady earning a great deal of money.

Joyce   So what's that got to do with you at the age of seventeen?

Marlene   Just because you were married and had somewhere to live –

Joyce   You could have lived at home. / Or live with me

Marlene   Don't be stupid.

Joyce   and Frank. / You said you weren't keeping it. You

Marlene   You never suggested.

Joyce   shouldn't have had it / if you wasn't going to keep it.

Marlene   Here we go.

Joyce   You was the most stupid, / for someone so clever you was the most stupid, get yourself pregnant, not go to the doctor, not tell.

Marlene   You wanted it, you said you were glad, I remember the day, you said I'm glad you never got rid of it, I'll look after it, you said that down by the river. So what are you saying, sunshine, you don't want her?

Joyce   Course I'm not saying that.

Marlene   Because I'll take her, / wake her up and pack now.

Joyce   You wouldn't know how to begin to look after her.

Marlene Don't you want her?

Joyce Course I do, she's my child.

Marlene Then what are you going on about / why did I have her?

Joyce You said I got her off you / when you didn't –

Marlene I said you were lucky / the way it –

Joyce Have a child now if you want one. You're not old.

Marlene I might do.

Joyce Good.

Pause.

Marlene I've been on the pill so long / I'm probably sterile.

Joyce Listen when Angie was six months I did get pregnant and I lost it because I was so tired looking after your fucking baby / because she cried so much – yes I did tell

Marlene You never told me.

Joyce you – / and the doctor said if I'd sat down all day with

Marlene Well I forgot.

Joyce my feet up I'd've kept it / and that's the only chance I ever had because after that –

Marlene I've had two abortions, are you interested? Shall I tell you about them? Well I won't, it's boring, it wasn't a problem. I don't like messy talk about blood / and what a bad

Joyce If I hadn't had your baby. The doctor said.

Marlene time we all had. I don't want a baby. I don't want to talk about gynaecology.

Joyce Then stop trying to get Angie off of me.

Marlene I come down here after six years. All night you've been saying I don't come often enough. If I don't come for another six years she'll be twenty-one, will that be OK?

Joyce   That'll be fine, yes, six years would suit me fine.

Pause.

Marlene   I was afraid of this.

I only came because I thought you wanted . . .

I just want . . .

Marlene *cries*.

Joyce   Don't grizzle, Marlene, for God's sake.

Marly? Come on, pet. Love you really.

Fucking stop it, will you?

Marlene   No, let me cry. I like it.

They laugh, **Marlene** *begins to stop crying*.

I knew I'd cry if I wasn't careful.

Joyce   Everyone's always crying in this house. Nobody takes any notice.

Marlene   You've been wonderful looking after Angie.

Joyce   Don't get carried away.

Marlene   I can't write letters but I do think of you.

Joyce   You're getting drunk. I'm going to make some tea.

Marlene   Love you.

Joyce *gets up to make tea*.

Joyce   I can see why you'd want to leave. It's a dump here.

Marlene   So what's this about you and Frank?

Joyce   He was always carrying on, wasn't he? And if I wanted to go out in the evening he'd go mad, even if it was nothing, a class, I was going to go to an evening class. So he had this girlfriend, only twenty-two poor cow, and I said go on, off you go, hoppit. I don't think he even likes her.

Marlene   So what about money?

Joyce   I've always said I don't want your money.

Marlene   No, does he send you money?

Joyce   I've got four different cleaning jobs. Adds up. There's not a lot round here.

Marlene   Does Angie miss him?

Joyce   She doesn't say.

Marlene   Does she see him?

Joyce   He was never that fond of her to be honest.

Marlene   He tried to kiss me once. When you were engaged.

Joyce   Did you fancy him?

Marlene   No, he looked like a fish.

Joyce   He was lovely then.

Marlene   Ugh.

Joyce   Well I fancied him. For about three years.

Marlene   Have you got someone else?

Joyce   There's not a lot round here. Mind you, the minute you're on your own, you'd be amazed how your friends' husbands drop by. I'd sooner do without.

Marlene   I don't see why you couldn't take my money.

Joyce   I do, so don't bother about it.

Marlene   Only got to ask.

Joyce   So what about you? Good job?

Marlene   Good for a laugh. / Got back from the US of A a bit

Joyce   Good for more than a laugh I should think.

Marlene   wiped out and slotted into this speedy employment agency and still there.

Joyce   You can always find yourself work then.

Marlene   That's right.

Joyce   And men?

Marlene   Oh there's always men.

Joyce   No one special?

Marlene   There's fellas who like to be seen with a high-flying lady. Shows they've got something really good in their pants. But they can't take the day to day. They're waiting for me to turn into the little woman. Or maybe I'm just horrible of course.

Joyce   Who needs them?

Marlene   Who needs them? Well I do. But I need adventures more. So on on into the sunset. I think the eighties are going to be stupendous.

Joyce   Who for?

Marlene   For me. / I think I'm going up up up.

Joyce   Oh for you. Yes, I'm sure they will.

Marlene   And for the country, come to that. Get the economy back on its feet and whoosh. She's a tough lady, Maggie.[42] I'd give her a job. / She just needs to hang in there. This country

Joyce   You voted for them, did you?

Marlene   needs to stop whining. / Monetarism is not stupid.[43]

Joyce   Drink your tea and shut up, pet.

Marlene   It takes time, determination. No more slop. / And

Joyce   Well I think they're filthy bastards.

42 Marlene is talking about Margaret Thatcher, the British prime minister at the time. For more information, see the commentary section on this topic.

43 Monetarism is an economic theory, most closely associated with the American economist Milton Friedman, which was adopted by Margaret Thatcher's Conservative government and, concurrently, by Ronald Reagan's US presidential administration. Both regimes used monetarist policies in an attempt to boost their economies and control rates of inflation (the rate at which prices rise over time causing the devaluation of currency) by reducing the rate at which money was supplied to the economy in the form of public spending (government investment in public services). These policies had some extremely negative social consequences, particularly within poorer communities, such as Joyce's.

Marlene   who's got to drive it on? First woman prime minister. Terrifico. Aces. Right on. / You must admit. Certainly gets my vote.

Joyce   What good's first woman if it's her? I suppose you'd have liked Hitler if he was a woman. Ms Hitler. Got a lot done, Hitlerina. / Great adventures.

Marlene   Bosses still walking on the workers' faces? Still Dadda's little parrot? Haven't you learned to think for yourself? I believe in the individual. Look at me.

Joyce   I am looking at you.

Marlene   Come on, Joyce, we're not going to quarrel over politics.

Joyce   We are though.

Marlene   Forget I mentioned it. Not a word about the slimy unions will cross my lips.[44]

Pause.

Joyce   You say Mother had a wasted life.

Marlene   Yes I do. Married to that bastard.

Joyce   What sort of life did he have? / Working in the fields like

Marlene   Violent life?

Joyce   an animal. / Why wouldn't he want a drink?

Marlene   Come off it.

Joyce   You want a drink. He couldn't afford whisky.

Marlene   I don't want to talk about him.

---

44   Marlene is referring to trade unions, who protect workers' rights through advocacy and representation. Some employers, such as Marlene, and politicians, such as Thatcher, who value the advancement of the economy over the rights of workers, believe unions are too powerful, hence Marlene's derogatory language here. Thatcher famously sought to disempower trade unions, for example, through her aggressive handling of the 1984–5 Miners' Strike.

Joyce   You started, I was talking about her. She had a rotten life because she had nothing. She went hungry.

Marlene   She was hungry because he drank the money. / He used to hit her.

Joyce   It's not all down to him. / Their lives were rubbish. They

Marlene   She didn't hit him.

Joyce   were treated like rubbish. He's dead and she'll die soon and what sort of life / did they have?

Marlene   I saw him one night. I came down.

Joyce   Do you think I didn't? / They didn't get to America and

Marlene   I still have dreams.

Joyce   drive across it in a fast car. / Bad nights, they had bad days.

Marlene   America, America, you're jealous. / I had to get out,

Joyce   Jealous?

Marlene   I knew when I was thirteen, out of their house, out of them, never let that happen to me, / never let him, make my own way, out.

Joyce   Jealous of what you've done, you're ashamed of me if I came to your office, your smart friends, wouldn't you, I'm ashamed of you, think of nothing but yourself, you've got on, nothing's changed for most people / has it?

Marlene   I hate the working class / which is what you're going

Joyce   Yes you do.

Marlene   to go on about now, it doesn't exist any more, it means lazy and stupid. / I don't like the way they talk. I don't

Joyce   Come on, now we're getting it.

Marlene   like beer guts and football vomit and saucy tits / and brothers and sisters –

Joyce   I spit when I see a Rolls Royce, scratch it with my ring /
Mercedes it was.

Marlene   Oh very mature –

Joyce   I hate the cows I work for / and their dirty dishes with
blanquette of fucking veau.[45]

Marlene   and I will not be pulled down to their level by a flying
picket and I won't be sent to Siberia / or a loony bin[46]

Joyce   No, you'll be on a yacht, you'll be head of Coca-Cola and
you wait, the eighties is going to be stupendous all right because
we'll get you lot off our backs –

Marlene   just because I'm original. And I support Reagan even if
he is a lousy movie star because the reds are swarming up his map
and I want to be free in a free world –[47]

Joyce   What? / What?

Marlene   I know what I mean / by that – not shut up here.

45 Blanquette de veau is a French dish of veal, cooked in a white sauce. Joyce sees this
complicated dish, made with expensive ingredients, as indicative of the pretentious wealth
displayed by the women for whom she cleans.

46 One tactic used by trade unions is the practice of 'striking' (withdrawing labour) until
workers' demands are met. Striking workers often form a 'picket' line outside their place of
work to publicize their cause and discourage their colleagues from working (and thus
undermining their strike action). A 'flying picket' is a group of trade union supporters
prepared to travel to different locations to support other workers' strikes. This practice (also
known as 'secondary picketing') was made illegal by Thatcher's government.

   Being 'sent to Siberia' is a turn of phrase that references the practice employed by
communist Russia (also known as the USSR or Soviet Union) of sending those who
disagreed with the political regime to brutal prison camps (known as gulags) in the freezing
north of the country. The comparison this draws between the attitudes of British trade
unions in the 1980s and Soviet communism in the early to mid-twentieth century is clearly
hyperbolic, but was not an uncommon slur to be made at this time.

47 Marlene admires the US President Ronald Reagan, who was an ally of Thatcher and had
similar policies. Before becoming president, Reagan had had a career in Hollywood.
Communists were also referred to as 'reds' (the colour associated with their movement and
flag). As well as his strained relationship with the Soviet Union, Reagan also feared the
communist movements in Central and South America (the ones Marlene describes as
'swarming up his map'), and consequently provided support to a number of brutal
anti-communist regimes.

Joyce   So don't be round here when it happens because if someone's kicking you I'll just laugh.

Silence.

Marlene   I don't mean anything personal. I don't believe in class. Anyone can do anything if they've got what it takes.

Joyce   And if they haven't?

Marlene   If they're stupid or lazy or frightened, I'm not going to help them get a job, why should I?

Joyce   What about Angie?

Marlene   What about Angie?

Joyce   She's stupid, lazy and frightened, so what about her?

Marlene   You run her down too much. She'll be all right.

Joyce   I don't expect so, no. I expect her children will say what a wasted life she had. If she has children. Because nothing's changed and it won't with them in.

Marlene   Them, them. / Us and them?

Joyce   And you're one of them.

Marlene   And you're us, wonderful us, and Angie's us / and Mum and Dad's us.

Joyce   Yes, that's right, and you're them.

Marlene   Come on, Joyce, what a night. You've got what it takes.

Joyce   I know I have.

Marlene   I didn't really mean all that.

Joyce   I did.

Marlene   But we're friends anyway.

Joyce   I don't think so, no.

Marlene   Well it's lovely to be out in the country. I really must make the effort to come more often.

I want to go to sleep.

I want to go to sleep.

Joyce *gets blankets for the sofa.*

Joyce   Goodnight then. I hope you'll be warm enough.

Marlene   Goodnight. Joyce –

Joyce   No, pet. Sorry.

Joyce *goes.*

Marlene *sits wrapped in a blanket and has another drink.*

Angie *comes in.*

Angie   Mum?

Marlene   Angie? What's the matter?

Angie   Mum?

Marlene   No, she's gone to bed. It's Aunty Marlene.

Angie   Frightening.

Marlene   Did you have a bad dream? What happened in it? Well you're awake now, aren't you pet?

Angie   Frightening.